Sensations
and
Phenomenology

Sensations
and
Phenomenology

HARMON M. CHAPMAN

Indiana University Press · Bloomington and London

CONTENTS

FOREWORD

The central theme of the following essay is that there are no such things as "sensations" or "impressions" in the traditional sense of modern epistemology. The assumption that there are such I call the "theory of sensation." Since the proof of non-existence is notoriously difficult, I offer instead an exposé partly historical, partly analytical. I attempt to show how the theory originated with Descartes, how at its inception it acquired two accessory theories, how in league with these it issued in an exciting new problem of knowledge and existence, how for this problem and its solutions the sensation theory prescribed the terms and conditions thus fixing the framework and ground rules for all who would philosophize in the "modern" vein, and how finally it persisted as a speculative tradition upwards of three centuries to the Transcendental Phenomenology of Edmund Husserl.

The essay culminates in an examination of Husserl's Phenomenology with its doctrine of transcendental constitution. In examining this doctrine I focus chiefly on its main support, the famous "reduction" or *epoché,* the suspending of existence. This suspension turns out to be a withholding of a mere "sense" of existing, which consciousness confers on objects of sense insofar as they are made ("constituted") of impressions. That the direct objects of sense are but complexes of impressions is of course a characteristic tenet of the sensation theory. The upshot is that this theory, silently and uncritically presupposed, underlies the whole of Husserl's transcendental phenomenology, rendering it to this extent unphenomenological, as it also rendered uncritical the critical philosophy of Immanuel Kant.

My mode of analysis is not that of current linguistic analysis. This latter has a devastating antiseptic power which might well have served my purpose. But it is quite foreign to the tradition I am examining, and I would prefer to criticize this tradition from within rather than from without. Hence I have chosen a mode of analysis more akin to its own native habits of thought. If I claim a right, even a responsibility, to proceed in this old-fashioned way, it is because I was reared in this tradition and am reluctant to turn upon it weapons of alien origin.

In adopting this procedure I am quite prepared to be found on occasion to ride roughshod over niceties and nuances of meaning which my friends in linguistic analysis will find objectionable. A further excuse is my synoptic aim, which has impelled me to draw boldly with a few broad strokes rather than minutely with a profusion of fine lines. This boldness has brought brevity, but it has also exposed me to the danger of being "positive"—it was *The New Yorker,* I think, which once defined "being positive" as "being wrong at the top of one's voice."

If I have been thus "positive," perhaps others more knowledgeable than I will be moved to rise in defense of the doctrines I here assail. I think first of all of Dorion Cairns, to whom I owe so much of what I know of Phenomenology, and of others like Quentin Lauer and Maurice Natanson. They, if anybody, could resolve the difficulties I encounter and thus render Phenomenology and American philosophy in general, not to mention myself, a notable service.

If there is anything original in this essay I am not aware of it. Novelty is not my concern. My concern is rather with the tradition of which I am a child even while trying also to be its critic. I am so steeped in this tradition that my thoughts seem to be its thoughts; each seems to echo a voice that has already spoken. My sense of obligation, accordingly, is so vast as to defy enumeration.

Only in a few instances can I acknowledge specific indebtedness. I have already mentioned Dorion Cairns. I must also mention two friends and colleagues, Raziel Abelson and Chauncey Downes, who read the manuscript and offered valuable suggestions. There are also Winifred and Leonard Carpenter, without whose gracious generosity this book would not have come to pass. There is yet another whose aid and encouragement were indispensable. How, in the midst of her many wifely and motherly duties, she managed to find the time to read and query, and reread and encourage, all with limitless patience, I shall never know. To these last three, especially to the memory of the first, I dedicate this volume, mindful that it is but the token of a gratitude that defies expression.

Now in *medias res!*

H. M. C.

University College
New York University

Sensations
and
Phenomenology

I
Two Fundamental Assumptions

Whitehead once advised, "When you are criticizing the philosophy of an epoch, do not chiefly direct your attention to those intellectual positions which its exponents feel it necessary explicitly to defend. There will be some fundamental assumptions which adherents of all the variant systems within the epoch unconsciously presuppose."* Because they are presupposed, more or less unconsciously, these assumptions are seldom if ever mentioned; they are simply taken for granted, like the air we breathe. Yet, because they are fundamental, they are always present, constituting—again like the air we breathe—what might be called the atmosphere of an epoch.

One of the fundamental assumptions which characterize the epoch known as "modern philosophy" is the notion of "sensation" or "sense impression." This notion takes it for granted that in all sense perception there occur inside the perceiving subject, as a consequence of the stimulation of his sense organs, private sensations or impressions corresponding to the sensible qualities perceived: visual sensations corresponding to the colors we perceive with our eyes, auditory sensations corresponding to the

*Quoted in W. K. C. Guthrie, The Greek Philosophers (New York: Harper, 1950), p. 11.

3

sounds we hear with our ears, tactual sensations corresponding to the qualities we perceive by touch, olfactory sensations corresponding to the odors we smell, and gustatory sensations corresponding to the flavors we taste—to mention only the five traditional senses.

The notion goes further than this. It holds that the sensation not only corresponds to the perceived quality; it actually *is* this quality *as perceived.* For the quality *as perceived,* as the immediate sensory content of the perception, is private to the perceiver and hence must be one with the sensation itself. Naturally, something must be added or done to the private sensation so that what originally occurs as an inner impression can be perceived as a public quality.

One thing more: sensations are "inner" in exactly the same sense as aches and pains and ticklings and kinesthetic sensations. These are all "sensations" in a wider sense, consorting together as subjective contents of our stream of consciousness. Only those sensations, however, which are also sense impressions, i.e., derive somehow from our sense organs, are acted upon by the mind so as to be perceived as outer qualities of things; the others are not.

Sensation in this sense is manifestly not a simple notion; it is rather a theory, whose central tenet is that the sensuous qualities of external things are really but internal sensations in the perceiving mind. This is the "theory of sensation" which I propose to study in the following pages. The theory itself was first set forth by Descartes and by him made the starting point of an exciting new philosophic venture. At the hands of Descartes's successors, however, the theory quickly lost its status as a theory and became almost at once one of those fundamental assumptions which, as Whitehead remarked, come to be more or less unconsciously presupposed by the exponents of an epoch. What happened here is that the theory *as theory* "went underground," so to speak, or became so "sedimented" in the term "sensation"—also in the term "idea," as we shall see shortly—that it rarely thereafter came explicitly to utterance. My aim is to bring it to utterance and to examine it carefully, in a systematic and historical vein.

Having uncovered the central tenet or thesis of the theory, that the sensuous qualities of sense objects are really but subjective sensations in the perceiving mind, let us see what is further involved.

First to be noted is that the thesis rests on a distinction between two kinds of qualities or properties which all things appear to possess on becoming objects of sense perception. There are 1) those qualities which may be called "sensible" because they are associated directly and uniquely with our various organs of sense: colors with the eyes; sounds with the ears; smoothness with touch; odors with the nose; and flavors with the tongue. In contrast with these sensible qualities there are 2) what may be called the mathematical properties of external things: shape, size, weight, position, motion, number, and the like, no one of which is confined, like the sensible qualities, to one organ or department of sense. On the contrary, these mathematical properties would seem to be quite independent of any of our senses; for when one or more of our senses fail, as they occasionally do with heavy colds or old age, then things "lose" their odors and flavors, or their colors and sounds, but never their mathematical properties. These latter would thus seem to be independent of our senses, whereas the sensible qualities would seem to be altogether dependent.

This distinction between the sensible qualities of things and their mathematical properties is better known to us, in terms made famous by John Locke, as that between the "secondary qualities" and the "primary qualities" of external objects, the secondary being the sensible qualities, the primary being the mathematical qualities. I shall prefer the more familiar Lockean version, but with the clear understanding that it signifies nothing more than what has so far been explicitly stated, that the secondary qualities are dependent on our sense organs, the primary qualities not.

Plainly the theory of sensation assumes or presupposes this distinction between the primary and secondary qualities of empirical things. But just as plainly it also assumes something more. For in declaring that the secondary qualities are but "subjective" sensations inside our minds, the sensation theory is going well beyond the distinction; it is "subjectivizing" the secondary qualities, or "reducing" them to sensations. Now since it is by this subjectivizing reduction that we pass from the distinction to the theory, plainly the distinction must be prior to the theory and independent of it; so that one may hold to the distinction between primary and secondary qualities without subscribing to the theory of sensation.

The reason for this subjectivizing reduction I shall examine later on. Here I wish only to point out that it leads from the distinction to the very important thesis that the secondary qualities are not really qualities of outer things at all, but actually only subjective impressions, sensations, "ideas," sense data inside the perceiving mind or consciousness. Taken at its face value—and it is meant to be taken literally—this is an astonishing utterance at which common sense can only stand agape. For what it says is that the color of eyes, the sound of voices, the softness and warmth of flesh, the fragrance of flowers, the flavor of foods, in short, *all* the sensible qualities which things possess for us in our daily lives, by which they are identified and sought or shunned, are not really "out there" attaching to things, but private sensations inside our minds. If common experience, the only experience we have, is to be trusted, this is simply incomprehensible. For what experience reveals is precisely the opposite: that these sensible qualities of things are not "in the mind," but "out there" in things themselves; and, indeed, so fused with primary qualities —colors with shapes and motions, sounds with distances and directions, hardness with surfaces and edges—that the two kinds of qualities would seem to be utterly inseparable in fact even though distinguishable in thought. By no effort can we perceive things otherwise than as possessing both primary and secondary qualities. And by no effort can we perceive things otherwise than by our organs of sense. Moreover, since it is by the same organs of sense that we perceive both primary and secondary qualities, must not the primary qualities be in a way just as "sensible" as the secondary, and in a similar way just as sense-dependent?

Plainly the evidence of experience is that the primary and secondary qualities *as perceived* are inseparable and are on precisely the same footing, as Berkeley rightly insisted. This, however, is not to deny a certain difference between them *as qualities of objects*. Experience confirms this difference or distinction—up to a point. But to what point? This question, too, I shall defer. My concern here is with the evidence of experience which confirms, up to an unspecified point, the distinction between primary and secondary qualities, but does not confirm the thesis of the sensation theory. Experience flatly opposes the separation of the qualities which this theory entails and the subjectivizing of the secondary.

Because experience opposes the theory, the theory in its turn must oppose experience; it must discredit experience. This it does by calling experience "naive," "uncritical," the source of "naive realism." Every student of philosophy soon learns that to be naive or uncritical about direct experience and its evidence is to be unphilosophical and that naive realism is intellectually disreputable. For, plainly, *if* direct experience is a matter of private sensations, its evidence must be equally private and—to this extent, at least—unacceptable. But this "if" is just the point at issue, the point where experience in its common-sense capacity opposes the theory of sensation. For the theory, however, this is no issue at all; it is simply beyond question, axiomatically evident, that experience begins with subjective sensations.

And so the theory of sensation, serenely confident of its critical ascendancy, was moved to dispense with naive experience and to resort to "reason" alone. Under the guidance of reason the theory burgeoned in a brilliant display of metaphysics. At the hands of Descartes and his immediate successors this metaphysical outburst flared up and then partly subsided, leaving as a residue another one of those "fundamental assumptions" of which Whitehead spoke. This second predilection I shall call "monadism," for reasons now to be related.

It all began with Descartes, who saw at once that his new theory of sensation had in tow two metaphysical corollaries. The first of these corollaries is that external things literally possess only primary qualities, that the external world is literally an insensible, mathematical reality—a *res extensa* (extended thing or substance), as Descartes called it—utterly devoid of all secondary qualities. This notion was of great importance to Descartes, for he was confident that only if the world were a *res extensa* could it be a proper object for the new mathematical approach to nature. We have dropped Descartes's term but retained its sense in our notion of the "physical world," which means the world just as it is depicted by natural science. Notice that this "physical world"—or *res extensa*—is not merely an aspect or facet of a richer empirical world of experience; it is not this "richer" world shorn, for methodological reasons only, of its sensible vestments. Rather it *is* the empirical world as it really, metaphysically is, just as it is disclosed to the initiates of natural science. In this "scientific" world the secondary qualities have no possible place, not even in our sense organs or brains, for these too are "physical" objects and possess only primary qualities. The secondary qualities have been read out of the world altogether and must find lodging elsewhere. The most obvious place is the human mind.

The second metaphysical corollary is that the human mind is the lodging place of the secondary qualities, and hence must be a substance completely different from *res extensa,* as different as the nonextended or nonspatial from the extended or spatial, as that which thinks from that which cannot think. The mind on this assumption must exist by itself quite outside the physical world, and must be as closed to this world, and as self-contained, as the world is to it. Indeed, it must be a kind of inner world of intangible "ideas" over against the outer world of tangible things. Descartes called it a *res cogitans* (thinking thing or substance), to contrast it as sharply as possible with *res extensa.*

The important point here is the contrast between *res cogitans* and *res extensa.* This contrast is so extreme that it can hardly be exaggerated. With it Descartes introduced into modern philosophy an unparalleled opposition or "dualism," a metaphysical split so final, so absolute, so unbridgeable, that it destroys the very possibility of the severed members forming a single metaphysical whole. No real togetherness is possible between *res cogitans* and *res extensa;* they have no possible meeting ground. Hence they can form not one ultimate whole, but two separate wholes—two at the very least. The successors of Descartes found this intolerable and set about trying to overcome the dualism, trying to find beneath the dualism a conciliating unity (monism). One thinks at once of Spinoza's parallelism, of the idealisms of Leibnitz, Berkeley, Kant, Hegel, of the materialism of Hobbes and Marx—to mention but a conspicuous few.

This "revolt against dualism" is perhaps the dominant metaphysical theme in modern philosophy. From Spinoza to the present it recurs without sign of abating. It recurs because that which it opposes persists, because the dualism which Descartes introduced has become one of the pivotal centers on which modern philosophy turns, one of those fundamental assumptions which, like the theory of sensation, are unconsciously assumed by all who would philosophize in the modern vein. This assumption has no accepted designation, like "sensation"; and Descartes's terms, *res cogitans* and *res extensa,* have long been abandoned. Because it is so unprecedented and extreme I shall call the dualism not Cartesian, but "monadic"; and I shall call its tacit, yet common, acceptance "monadism."

Leibnitz, who introduced the term "monad" from the Greek (meaning "one" or "the one"), did not speak of nature as a monad; he confined the term to souls and minds. In applying it to nature as well, I am suggesting that if minds are monads, nature too must be a monad. My reason for saying this is that the basic sense of "monad," or an integral part thereof, is that of a closed, self-contained order "without windows," i.e., into which nothing can enter and from which nothing can escape, in a word, a "conservative system." Now we are quite accustomed to viewing nature as a conservative system; nearly every high school graduate has been told that the quantity of mass (or "matter") and energy in the universe is constant or conserved. Leibnitz is holding in effect that souls and minds are similarly conservative with respect to the sum total of their contents, sensations, ideas, and the like. All I am adding is that the two notions go inseparably together, that in separating mind and nature in the fashion of Descartes we are making both equally conservative, both equally "closed" to each other. Taking "monad" in this sense of complete closedness—with of course, some apologies to Leibnitz—then clearly if mind is a monad, nature is a monad—or, if you prefer, a counter-monad.

Obviously by "monadism" I do not mean an express adherence to the view that mind and nature are monads. Still less do I signify an acceptance of Leibnitz's celebrated theory of monads.

Monadism does not even involve the use of the word "monad"; the word may be quite unknown. Monadism is rather the deeply sedimented predilection which predisposes us all, or nearly all, to take it simply for granted that mind and nature, or more commonly "psychical" and "physical," signify two distinct and separate orders of existence, two monads. Thus the familiar term "physical nature"—a curious etymological redundance—almost invariably stands for an order utterly closed to psychical mind or consciousness. By almost universal consent things psychical or mental, being inaccessible to the methods of natural inquiry, have no place at all in the "objective" world of science. Conversely, things psychical or psychological comprise a (dubious) "subjective" realm from which things physical are with equal finality excluded. And so we have the familiar opposition of psychical and physical with its many variations, thought and extension, subjective and objective, subject and object, thought and things, mind and matter, soul and body, inner consciousness and outer object, self and other, value and fact, and so on—all expressing covertly one and the same "monadic" opposition between mind and nature which was first propounded by Descartes.

The important point here is the monadic nature of the opposition. The contrasting pairs just enumerated are as old as western thought. The members of each pair were early distinguished one from the other, and several were found to be in tension, even conflict. In a loose sense they are all "opposites"; and the members of each pair may be said to stand in a kind of "opposition." But in no instance, I believe, is the traditional opposition conceived in the Cartesian sense of utter separation and exclusion— "closedness," as I have called it, in the fashion of monads. This irreconcilability is what is new and Cartesian and modern. This is what lies at the core of monadism.

The hold of this monadic view on the modern mind is astonishing, and the more so when we look at it against the classical background from which it emerged. Consider for a moment the meanings of the terms "physical" and "psychical" prior to Descartes. The one derives from *physis,* which means "nature" (*natura* in Latin); the other derives from *psyche,* which means "soul" (*anima* or *animus* in Latin) and which we at times transliterate into English. Aristotle at the far end of the classical tradition could hold that man's *psyche* is in a way his *physis* (nature). St. Thomas at the nearer end, agreeing with Aristotle, could speak of an *influxus physicus* in the *psyche* or *anima*—a position unalterably opposed by Descartes's immediate successors. There is no such opposition here between physical and psychical as we find after the advent of the sensation theory and its metaphysical corollaries.

What happened here, terminologically, is that "physical" came to be virtually synonymous with "material." Matter, you will recall, had been liberated by Descartes from all involvement with "form" and proclaimed a substance in its own right, a *res extensa.* At the same time form—at least as mind or soul (*mens sive animus*)—was similarly liberated from matter and proclaimed a substance in its own right, a *res cogitans.* Form as accident disappeared in the distinction between primary and secondary qualities, becoming as primary the essential or defining predicates of matter, and reducing as secondary to subjective contents of mind, sensations. What little was left of form was tarred with the caption "occult quality" and read out of the new movement together with potency and act. Thus the classical union of "form" and "matter" as the polar constituents of substance was dissolved at a stroke and replaced with the brand new opposition and separation of incorporeal and corporeal substance.

It is easy to see in this opposition how "psychical" took its stand with incorporeal mind. It is not equally easy to see how "physical" took its stand with corporeal matter and became opposed to "psychical." The explanation, possibly, lies in the increasing use of "physical" to modify "world" as in the expression "physical world." On becoming a material substance the world, continuing to be designated as "physical," probably gave to "physical" the exclusive connotation of "material" or "corporeal." At all events, a vast terminological convulsion occurred in which a host of *distinctions* carefully refined and conciliated over the centuries was suddenly suppressed, transformed, and gathered up into one overriding metaphysical *opposition* and *separation,* the unbridgeable monadic dualism of psychical mind and physical nature.

All this is quite explicit with Descartes. He was fully aware that in subjectivizing the secondary qualities and separating them from the primary, the sensation theory was committed via its metaphysical corollaries to the unprecedented and irreconcilable opposition of *res cogitans* and *res extensa*. Descartes was not fully aware of the monadic nature of this opposition; he still held that mind and body could interact. Spinoza and Leibnitz corrected this at once. With them the dualism attained its sharpest formulation and then went underground, becoming one of those "fundamental assumptions" which characterize the modern outlook. On becoming thus implicit the dualism lost much of its sharpness, as do most tenets that come to be simply taken for granted. But for all its want of sharpness its edge is keenly felt in the predilection that psychical mind and physical nature are "closed" to each other, that never the twain shall meet and merge and form a real unity, comparable to the classical union of form and matter. To this "closed" theory of mind and nature I shall later oppose an "open" theory.

By way of summary, we have uncovered two "fundamental assumptions," two of the most powerful in the framework of modern thought. The more basic of the two is the theory of sensation, inasmuch as it gave rise to monadism. This priority is not manifest in their role as fundamental assumptions; they would seem to be rather coeval companions holding a joint sway. But they are not coeval in origin; the sensation theory is prior. Because it is prior, it is that on which our attention naturally comes principally to focus. The question now arises as to the origin of the sensation theory. What are its grounds? By what arguments and from what evidence does it derive? What, in a word, is its rationale?

In raising this question it is important to note once again that although the theory of sensation rests on the distinction between primary and secondary qualities, it is not necessarily entailed by this distinction. The distinction is logically independent of the theory of sensation. To get from the distinction to the theory a further assumption must be made; the secondary qualities must be subjectivized. If we refrain from making this assumption, we may then hold to the distinction, as every thoughtful scientist must, without subscribing to the theory. In this event, the distinction is taken not as a philosophic gambit but as a methodological aid to natural inquiry. It was so taken by Kepler and Galileo. They did not use it to support a philosophic theory of sensation. Nor did anybody else before Descartes. It was Descartes, and Descartes alone, who first gave to the world the theory of sensation. It is for this reason that I speak of the theory as "Cartesian" and its attendant monadism as "modern."

I stress this point, for as legatees of Descartes we are not in the habit of regarding the distinction as independent—both logically and chronologically—of the theory; we tend to forget that there was a time when the distinction was drawn without any thought of the theory. In our Cartesian heritage the two are so closely associated that the bare mention of the distinction calls at once to mind the theory of subjectivity. Even such excellent historians as Cassirer and Burtt—to mention but two of many—simply take it for granted that when Kepler and Galileo distinguish between primary and secondary qualities they are also proclaiming the "subjectivity" of the latter. If by "subjective" Cassirer and Burtt mean what the word has come to mean only since Descartes, namely, that the secondary qualities are but sensations in the mind, then Kepler and Galileo proclaimed no such thing. This I shall attempt to show in the next chapter, after which I shall turn to Descartes's arguments for the theory of sensation.

II
Scientific Humanism: Kepler and Galileo

1. Scientific Humanism

Kepler and Galileo were not philosophers, but natural scientists who lived at a time when natural science was only aborning. What has become for us a stupendous and fateful reality was for them hardly more than a prospect, albeit the prospect of a grandiose venture unlike anything else in the history of man. It was to be a venture of discovery and conquest. Nature, like a vast new continent, lay spread out before them, abounding in riches to be had for the taking. Mathematics was to be the instrument of seizure. With this mighty weapon, itself but newly forged, the whole domain was to be explored and exploited for the benefit of all. Such in brief was the exhilarating prospect, known as "scientific humanism," which fired the authors of natural inquiry and ushered in the new era that was to follow.

Today scientific humanism seems to be hardly more than a memory. Promise has given way to fulfillment, and with fulfillment has come a sobering sense of reality, touched of late with a grimness which the founding fathers did not anticipate. With its many blessings the grand venture has also brought latterly the hideous threat of extinction. The threat expresses nothing inherent in the undertaking itself, rather a failure in its execution. The spoils of conquest were not shared by all, but reserved for a privileged few; arbitrary rules of eligibility were imposed—religious, political, economic—in violation of the spirit of the venture. Like a prophet of old, Karl Marx denounced this injustice and called down on our generation the wrath of the wronged. In world Communism these wronged have raised their fists and voices in a raucous demand for their share of the bounty. Slowly, painfully this latter-day "scourge of God" seems to be compelling our grudging compliance with the aforesaid spirit which gave to the undertaking from the outset its profoundly "humanistic" character of being for the benefit of all mankind.

On this understanding natural science is not inherently indifferent to human values; it is inherently relevant. It is not solely a method of natural inquiry, a vast accumulation of natural knowledge. It is also an attitude and way of life, a way of looking *at* the world and living *in* the world, an attitude which sets a supreme value on this life and its mundane course—*for all*.

Natural science was originally so conceived by its authors, and as so conceived has come to engage the minds and efforts of men and nations. Only where it is so conceived, that is, only where scientific humanism prevails, overtly or covertly, can natural science flourish. This is to say that scientific humanism is still the presiding aegis of natural science and must thrive to sustain its offspring. If this be so, then scientific humanism must be more than a lingering memory; it must be as real and present for us as it was for Galileo and Kepler. With its novelty worn off it must have gone underground, there to obtain, like the theory of sensation and monadism, as a "fundamental assumption."

But it is a unique kind of "assumption"; it is too wide and deep to be encased in a philosophic formula or article of belief. It is not a part of a framework, but a whole framework itself, a pervasive attitude, a comprehensive outlook, appealing as much to the emotions and the will as to the intellect. Let us note briefly some features of this attitude and its characteristic sense of value.

First, and perhaps most obviously, natural science is unique among the endeavors of man in the quality of its cooperation, in calling equally for individual and collective effort. In no other endeavor is there such a complete accord between individual accomplishment and group aggrandizement; in every instance a gain for one is a gain for all, and conversely. Also, in no other group are the admission requirements so general, so free from bias, so universal. Without regard to color, sex, creed, social status or political affiliation anyone may participate to the extent of his talents and training. "In no other endeavor have men with varied abilities, temperaments, and allegiances, cooperated so broadly, so persistently, or so successfully. Nowhere have the values of industry, honesty, imagination, self-criticism, and freedom from prejudice, been more brilliantly demonstrated." (Dorion Cairns in an unpublished paper.) Never have men so thoroughly cooperated; never have their labors been so richly rewarded—for the benefit of all. In this respect modern natural science is unique, without compare, among the endeavors of men.

To be or become all this, natural science did not require, like an office building, to be preceded by a detailed blueprint of itself. It grew, rather, like a living thing, animated by scientific humanism. Not being the architect of natural science, but rather its elan vital, scientific humanism did not offer itself or its program as a philosophy, still less as a theology, and hence did not seek expression in the form of a doctrine. Without bible or textbook, scientific humanism came to utterance and propagated itself more by deeds than by words. Such words as it did employ

—and it was movingly articulate—were chiefly incitements and guides to action. The action contemplated had a single end: the conquest of nature for the benefit of all.

The conquest of nature! Never before had such a notion taken hold in the western world. It was no article of the Christian faith and no tenet of classical philosophy. For the Christian the world was but the dark anteroom to salvation, and for the Greek an object to be known, without thought of mastery. Only the ancient Hebrews had entertained the thought of mastery. And they propounded it seriously. For them it was the very first of the divine commandments. No sooner had God created human beings, than He blessed them and said unto them, "Be fruitful, and multiply, and replenish the earth, and subdue it" (Gen., 1:28). The injunction is repeated after the flood (Gen., 9). And it moves the Psalmist to the most amazing outburst. When he cries "What is man, that thou art mindful of him?" it is not from a humbling sense of man's inconsequence, but from an exalted sense of his near divinity. "For thou hast made him a little lower than God [Elohim, hence not "angels" as the King James version modestly but incorrectly renders it] and hast crowned him with glory and honor. Thou madest him to have dominion over the works of thy hands; thou hast put all things under his feet" (Ps., 8:4-6). For sheer boldness of conception and utterance I know of nothing to match these words. They are startling even today. And what a glow they add to the prosaic talk of "prediction and control"! Note also that this mandate of dominion was issued to man as man, that it was in his capacity as a human being—not as Jew or Gentile—that he was "divinely elected" to the exalted office of master of creation. Scientific humanism could hardly aspire to a higher sanction—or point up more forcibly the neglect of the first of all the divine commandments.

Even newer in this vision was the idea that mathematics was to be the instrument of dominion. The Pythagoreans had regarded mathematics as a key to a kind of speculative understanding of nature and had deigned to apply it to such phenomena as the motions of the planets and the concordant intervals in music, giving rise to astronomy and harmony. But they eschewed the notion of a general application of mathematics to natural phenomena, especially if it bore any prospect of being useful; this was for shopkeepers, not philosophers. This disdain is well expressed by Plutarch in his life of the Roman general, Marcellus, who captured Syracuse. Archimedes, Plutarch tells us, had contrived some machines "not as matters of any importance, but as mere amusements in geometry"—at the urging of his kinsman, King Hiero of Syracuse. After a vivid account of the effectiveness of these machines in repulsing Marcellus's assaults by land and water, Plutarch adds, "Yet Archimedes possessed so high a spirit, so profound a soul, and such treasures of scientific knowledge, that though these inventions had now obtained him the renown of more than human sagacity, he yet would not deign to leave behind him any commentary or writing on such subjects; but, repudiating as sordid and ignoble the whole trade of engineering, and every sort of art that lends itself to mere use and profit, he placed his whole affection and ambition in those purer speculations where there can be no reference to the vulgar needs of life."

Compare this with Bacon's roughly parallel remarks in the Preface to his *Instauratio Magna*. Man is so completely encompassed by nature that "what he does and what he knows is only what he has observed of nature's order in fact or in thought; beyond this he knows nothing and can do nothing. For the chain of causes cannot by any force be loosed or broken, nor can nature be commanded except by being obeyed. And so those twin objects, *human knowledge* and *human power,* do really meet in one; and it is from ignorance of causes that operation fails" (Bacon's italics).

The tremendous change which has come over the thinking of

men could hardly be more dramatically put than by these two aristocrats of their respective cultures. For the one, knowledge is pure *theoria,* contemplation, in lofty detachment. For the other, knowledge is power of operation in close application to the vulgar facts of life. It makes no difference that Bacon failed to recognize the role of mathematics in the new knowledge of nature. He saw clearly what the new knowledge was aiming at and spoke for all when he stressed its practicality.

New, too, and finally, was the idea that the "fruits," as Bacon called them, of this new knowledge were to benefit all mankind, to mend the fabric of man's earthly existence. In the same Preface Bacon insists that "the matter in hand is no mere felicity of speculation, but the real business and fortunes of the human race, and all power of operation." In his *New Atlantis* he pictures vividly the promised "relief of man's estate," the mitigating of human sufferings and the multiplying of human comforts—for all, here and now.

The emphasis in this humanistic vision is unmistakably universalistic and secular, and just as unmistakably a reproof to the old order. The classical Greek ideal, with its lofty speculations for the leisured few, had no room for all mankind. And the Christian, meditating on life eternal, could take but little thought for the secular. Such thought as he did take was largely negative. For to the extent that salvation required forsaking "the world, the flesh, and the devil," the Christian attitude toward the secular was bound to be one of studied disengagement and neglect; to the extent that it fixed on the depravity of man, the Church could become the portal of salvation only by becoming the escape hatch from the world. In advocating flight rather than dominion, the Christian tradition virtually renounced the world as the tragic scene of man's fall from grace, and remanded it to the devil.

Against this denigration of the secular a massive protest was gathering in the minds and hearts of men. Had this protest been

more articulate it would have entered the theological battles of
the time and engaged both contending parties, Catholic and Protestant alike. Against both it would have inveighed that the negative Christian attitude toward creation was tantamount to 1)
damning as evil what the Creator in the process of creating had
six times found "good," the seventh time "very good," and 2)
violating flagrantly the first commandment to "be fruitful and
multiply, and replenish the earth, and subdue it."

But the protest was not thus articulate; it did not press directly
for doctrinal formulation, not even for Scriptural vindication. Being a vast transvaluation it spread more by infection than by argument and broke out not so much in opposition to salvation and
the Church as in favor of dominion and natural inquiry. This was
as it should be, for the new attitude was not primarily negative
and protestant, but positive and affirmative of values long neglected. Thus with its syndromes of secularism and universalism,
the new attitude found what expression it needed in the call to
dominion under the banner of scientific humanism—a call to
the greatest and noblest of crusades.

The point of this divigation is that scientific humanism was not
in the first instance a philosophy, but a whole new outlook on
life and nature and a new program of living by conquest. It was a
call, therefore, not to words but to action. As Bacon put it, the
matter in hand was "not an opinion to be held, but a work to be
done," a work of unprecedented magnitude calling for an unprecedented effort on the part of men individually and collectively.
The call obviously cut across religious, theological, philosophical,
national lines, across all lines in fact that divide men from one
another. Without regard to their divergent beliefs and loyalties
men everywhere were now invited to share in a mighty enterprise
from which all could profit.

It was while engaged in this enterprise that Kepler the Protestant and Galileo the Catholic drew their celebrated distinction

between primary and secondary qualities. For them the distinction was not philosophical and theoretical, but scientific and practical, a device for facilitating the application of mathematics to natural phenomena. Thus in spite of its philosophic implications—and for us they are many—the distinction remained for these authors of natural science essentially an *obiter dictum,* a means of clearing away obstructions and getting along with the work in hand. They were content, therefore, to leave to others the controversial task of elaborating its philsophic import.

2. *Kepler*

Kepler's version of the distinction turns on the notions of quantity and quality, the first two of Aristotle's categories of accident. Kepler contrasts his own view with that of Aristotle. Aristotle, he says, tended to regard the qualitative accidents of things as the more fundamental, whereas he, Kepler, regards the quantitative as the more fundamental. The quantitative determinations of things are prior to the qualitative in two respects. They are prior 1) in things and 2) in knowledge. They are prior in things in that they underlie the sensible qualities; they are the underlying, nonsensible elements of order, regularity, "harmony," such as he found, for example, in optics, music, and mechanics. Of this wonderful and pervasive "harmony of the world" (*harmonices mundi*) the sensible qualities are only signs or indices, mere effects which only half reveal their causes. The quantitative accidents are prior in knowledge because they are the proper objects of mind. "Just as the eye was made to see colors, and the ear to hear sounds, so the human mind was made to understand, not whatever you please, but quantity."* This is attested by the fact that mathematics, the

---

*Quoted in Edwin A. Burtt, Metaphysical Foundations of Physics, p. 57. In this account of Kepler and Galileo I also lean heavily on Ernst Cassirer, *Erkenntnis Problem,* Vol. 1.

most illustrious product of the human mind, is the great discipline of quantity in general. It is by mathematics, therefore, that the hidden harmony of the cosmos in all its quantitative variations is to be discovered and understood.

This dual priority of the quantitative over the qualitative and the marvelous conformity of the human mind to the mathematical nature of things are for Kepler manifest evidences of divine providence. Kepler's religious fervor verged on the extreme. He was intensely aware of the world as the handiwork of God; and he could have said a resounding "amen" to Galileo's contention that God's primary revelation lay in the great mathematical book of nature. Although he was a Protestant, Kepler was not deeply concerned with the reform of the Church or with refinements of doctrine. His concern was with the reform of our natural knowledge and with the refinements of natural inquiry. In this concern he spoke a common language with his Catholic contemporaries and could count on their ready assent to his own proclamations that God created the world in accordance with mathematical harmonies, that He ever geometrizes, that in making man in His own image God so designed the human mind that it should know primarily quantity.

There is philosophy in this, and metaphysics and theology and religion. But it is a mosaic of utterances almost without texture, without regard for the niceties of formulation and consistency. It is but a backdrop to the central action: the application of mathematics to natural phenomena. And since Kepler's heart was set on this central action he was content to leave the backdrop as it was. He was a natural scientist, not a philosopher or theologian.

3. Galileo

Galileo's version of the distinction is more incisive than Kepler's and marks an advance in the direction of Descartes. Indeed, it is so close to Descartes that we post-Cartesians are almost bound to read Descartes into it. A careful perusal, however, should suffice to persuade us that there is still a wide gap between Galileo and Descartes. To this end I shall reproduce here in part Burtt's excellent translation of the pertinent passage in Galileo's *Il Saggiatore,* which first appeared in 1623.*

But first I want to propose some examination of that which we call heat, whose generally accepted notion comes very far from the truth if my serious doubts be correct, inasmuch as it is supposed to be a true accident, affection, and quality really residing in the thing which we perceive (*sentire*) to be heated. Nevertheless I say, that indeed I feel myself impelled by the necessity, as soon as I conceive a piece of matter or corporeal substance, of conceiving that in its own nature it is bounded and figured in such and such a figure, that in relation to the others it is large or small, that it is in this or that place, in this or that time, that it is in motion or remains at rest, that it touches or does not touch another body, that it is single, few or many; in short by no imagination can a body be separated from such conditions: but that it must be white or red, bitter or sweet, sounding or mute, of a pleasant or unpleasant odor, I do not perceive my mind forced to acknowledge it necessarily accompanied by such conditions; so if the senses were not the escorts, perhaps the reason or the imagination by itself would never have arrived at them. Hence I think that these tastes, odors, colors, etc., on the side of the object in which they seem to us to exist, are nothing else than mere names, but hold their residence solely in the sensitive body; so that if the animal were removed, every such quality would be abolished and annihilated. Nevertheless, as soon as we have imposed names on them, particular and different from those of the other primary (*primi*) and real accidents, we induce ourselves to believe that they also exist just as truly and really as the latter. I think that by an illustration I can ex-

*Burtt, pp. 75f. My friend and colleague Professor Floyd Zulli assures me that this translation is quite adequate.

plain my meaning more clearly. I pass a hand, first over a
marble statue, then over a living man. Concerning all the
effects which come from the hand, as regards the hand itself, they are the same whether on the one or on the other
object—that is, these primary (*primi*) accidents, namely
motion and contact (for we call them by no other names)—
but the animate body which suffers that operation perceives
various affections according to the different parts touched,
and if the sole of the foot, the kneecap, or the armpit be
touched, it perceives besides the common contact, another
affection, to which we have given a particular name, calling
it tickling. Now this affection is all ours, and does not belong to the hand at all. And it seems to me that they would
greatly err who should say that the hand, besides motion
and contact, possessed in itself another faculty different
from those, namely the tickling faculty; so that tickling
would be an accident that exists in it.

This is Galileo at his best: a superb balance of evidence and
inference in support of an important conclusion. The conclusion
is that since mathematics grasps only the primary qualities of
things and since only the primary qualities of things are essential,
therefore, our mathematical knowledge of things is essential, i.e.,
genuine knowledge of nature. This may be "old hat" to us, but it
was not to Galileo and his contemporaries. They were accustomed
to expressing natural knowledge in the Aristotelian terms of substance, accident, form, genus and difference, act and potency.
Now of a sudden this is all to be swept aside and replaced by a
new vocabulary of motion expressed in the symbols of mathematics. The impact of this innovation must have been enormous.

Our interest here, however, is not in this conclusion or its
novelty, but in the argument itself and the view it takes of the
secondary qualities. They are not essential, i.e., they do not at-
tach to things as they are in themselves, but are only ascribed to
things by a sentient body which perceives them. When a sentient
body perceives anything by its senses, secondary qualities are

produced or caused in its sense organs by external causes which are moving bodies possessing only primary qualities. In this sense the secondary qualities exist only "in us," i.e., in our "animate and sensitive bodies," not in the things perceived. Hence if all animate and sensitive bodies were removed, and therewith all sense perception, all secondary qualities of things would also be removed and bodies would then be seen to possess only their essential primary qualities.

Notice that Galileo has not banished secondary qualities from the world. They exist for him in our objective sense organs, where they occur as objective effects of objective causes. Just because they are objective effects they can be used as "indices" of their causes. But as effects they cannot be ascribed to their causes as properties; and they obviously do not reside in all bodies since they are restricted in their occurrence to sensitive bodies only. Subjective is hardly the adjective to apply to them; for they are not mental entities, as opposed to physical, and hence not properly sensations or impressions or "ideas"; this is all to come later. "Relative" is the better adjective; for they are relative to our sense organs, fleeting in their occurrence, and inadequate, as effects, to characterize their causes. This is all that Galileo is saying about secondary qualities. This is enough, since it adequately prepares the way for applying mathematics to the primary causes which underlie the secondary qualities.

Thus Galileo, no more than Kepler, was advancing a new theory of sensation. The very notion of sensation, so familiar to us, was quite foreign to both Kepler and Galileo, indeed to all who preceded Descartes. The Latin words *sensatio* and *impressio* did not mean for them what the English words "sensation" and "impression" have come to mean for us, namely, a purely "subjective" sense datum residing wholly in the mind or consciousness. To be sure, the sensible qualities of things are for Galileo relative, fleeting effects. We would say at once that they are "subjective" with all that this implies. But this is not what Galileo said or meant. He did not "subjectivize" the secondary qualities. With the restraint of the disciplined inquirer he was attempting to draw an empirically grounded distinction between the primary and secondary qualities of things for the sovereign purpose of facilitating the application of mathematics to natural phenomena.

If Galileo did not go on to resolve the philosophic problems which his distinction raised, it was not because he was unaware of these problems or of the explosive threat which they posed to the scholastic notions then prevailing. It was because of his consuming interest in natural science. Now it is the good fortune of natural science that it does not have to wrestle with such problems philosophical; once its own needs are met it can blithely ignore them and resume its triumphant course. Galileo saw this clearly and with eminent good sense left these problems as he found them: as issues to confound the philosophers, not as roadblocks to impede natural inquiry.

What are the philosophic problems which the distinction between primary and secondary qualities raises? Perhaps the most obvious problem is this. If all bodies have only primary qualities, must not sentient bodies, as bodies, have only primary qualities? If so, how then can sentient bodies, any more than insentient bodies, offer sanctuary to secondary qualities? Another way of putting this is: how can any body possessing only primary qualities possess also the "quality" or "faculty" of sentience? For whatever sentience may be it is not a primary quality. Nor is it a secondary quality, although it involves secondary qualities. But how? Clearly the problem is not confined to bodies as bodies and their inherent qualities; it pertains also to the whole nature of sentience, of sense perception. If Galileo was aware of this problem he made no effort to solve it.

He did solve, however, another problem which is closely connected with the first. This problem we have already raised. What precisely is the difference between the two kinds of qualities? In declaring the secondary qualities to be but fleeting effects produced in our sense organs by more permanent primary causes, Galileo was saying that the two differ in the first instance as cause and effect and that the primary qualities enjoy the priority which usually attaches to the cause. But is it empirically evident that they differ as cause and effect?

If the question is one of empirical evidence, then I must urge once again the importance of the three observations which I made in the preceding chapter. 1) Primary and secondary qualities are so fused together as to be actually inseparable, so that although distinguishable in idea they are inseparable in fact. 2) They are both perceived "out there" in precisely the same sense as "objective" qualities of things, not as "residents" of our sense organs (and certainly not as "subjective" contents of our minds). 3) They are both perceived through the same organs of sense; it is only when these organs are stimulated that we perceive anything at all, and then always both primary and secondary qualities together; to this extent the primary qualities are just as "sensible" and sense-dependent as the secondary.

In the light of these three empirical observations it is definitely *not* empirically evident that primary and secondary qualities differ as cause and effect. But how then do they differ—granting that they actually do? It is not my intention here to answer this question, but to raise it, to insist on its importance in any philosophy of science, and to warn us that its answer is to be got not by hypothetical arguments, but by a careful analysis of such empirical data as are set forth in the three observations above. Only by analyzing and conciliating these inviolable matters of evidence can the distinction be clarified and rendered philosophically acceptable.

Galileo and Descartes were quite unaware of this need for clarification and hence were not inclined to any such program of

analysis and conciliation. The evidence they adduced was sufficient to persuade them that primary and secondary qualities differ
as cause and effect. In their eagerness they failed to note that
other evidence, equally pertinent, casts serious doubt on this difference. And so without further ado they adopted the distinction
as drawn, and used it each for his own purposes. Galileo used
it as a device to further the application of mathematics to nature.
Descartes saw in it a new theory of sensation (or "ideas") and
through this theory a pair of corollaries which called for a complete revision of human knowledge, a revision to be carried out
by that selfsame reason which was disporting itself so brilliantly
in the new mathematics and science. As Galileo was promoting a
new method of natural inquiry, Descartes was inaugurating a
new tradition of philosophy and prescribing for this tradition the
basic terms in which the central problem and its solution were to
be couched, those namely of the theory of sensation.

Had not Galileo distinguished primary from secondary qualities, as cause from effect, I strongly suspect that neither Descartes
nor anyone else would have thought of sensations. But as it was,
the distinction being given, Descartes extracted from it his momentous theory of sensation, not by analysis and conciliation, but
by argument and inference, in accordance with his own principles of "method." Let us now turn to Descartes's classic argument for sensations.

III

Descartes's Direct Argument for Sensations

Descartes's argument for sensations is set forth most forcibly in his *Principles of Philosophy,* Part IV. I shall quote in full two paragraphs from the translation by Haldane and Ross.*

CXCVII. That mind is of such a nature that from the motion of the body alone the various sensations can be excited in it.

It may, in the next place, be (easily) proved that our mind is of such a nature that the motions which are in the body are alone sufficient to cause it to have all sorts of thoughts, which do not give us any image of any of the motions which give rise to them; and specially that there may be excited in it those confused thoughts called feelings or sensations [*sensus, sive sensationes*]. For (first of all) we observe that words, whether uttered by the voice or merely written, excite in our minds all sorts of thoughts and emotions. On the same paper, with the same pen and ink, by moving the point of the pen ever so little over the paper in a certain way, we can trace letters which bring to the minds of our readers thoughts of battles, tempests or furies, and the emotions

*Cambridge University Press, 1931, Vol. 1, pp. 294-6.

of indignation and sadness; while if the pen be moved in another way, hardly different, thoughts may be given of quite a different kind, viz. those of quietude, peace, pleasantness, and the quite opposite passions of love and joy. Someone will perhaps reply that writing and speech do not immediately excite any passions in the mind, or imaginations of things different from the letters and sounds, but simply so to speak various acts of the understanding; and from these the mind, making them the occasion, then forms for itself the imaginations of a variety of things. But what shall we say of the sensations of what is painful and pleasurable? If a sword moved towards our body cuts it, from this alone pain results which is certainly not less different from the local movement of the sword or of the part of the body which is cut, than are color or sound or smell or taste. And therefore, as we see clearly that the sensation of pain is easily excited in us from the fact alone that certain parts of our body are locally disturbed by the contact with certain other bodies, we may conclude that our mind is of such a nature that certain local motions can excite in it all the affections belonging to all the other senses.

CXCVIII. That there is nothing known of external objects by the senses but their figure, magnitude or motion.

Besides this, we observe in the nerves no difference which may cause us to judge that some convey to the brain from the organs of the external sense any one thing rather than another, nor again that anything is conveyed there excepting the local motion of the nerves themselves. And we see that this local motion excites in us not alone the sensations of pleasure or pain, but also the sensations of sound and light. For if we receive a blow in the eye hard enough to cause the vibration to reach the retina, we see myriads of sparks which are yet not outside our eye; and when we place our finger on our ear to stop it, we hear a murmuring sound whose cause cannot be attributed to anything but the agitation of the air which is shut up within it. Finally we can likewise frequently observe that heat and the other sensible qualities, inasmuch as they are in objects, and also the forms of these bodies which are purely material, such as e.g. the forms of fire, are produced in them by the motions of certain other bodies, and that these again also produce other motions in other bodies. And we can very well conceive how the movement of one body can be caused by that of another, and diversified by the size, figure, and situation of its parts, but we can in nowise understand how these same things (viz. size, figure, and motion) can produce something entirely different in nature from themselves, such as are those substantial forms and real qualities which many suppose to exist in bodies; nor likewise can we understand how these forms or qualities possess the force adequate to cause motion in other bodies. But since we know that our mind is of such a nature that the diverse motions of body suffice to produce in it all the diverse sensations that it has, and as we see by experience that some of the sensations are really caused by such motions, though we do not find anything but these movements to pass through the organs of the external senses to the brain, we may conclude that we in no way likewise apprehend that in external objects like light, color, smell, taste, sound, heat, cold, and the other tactile qualities, or what we call their substantial forms, there is anything but the various dispositions of these objects which have the power of moving our nerves in various ways.

I shall never forget my first reading of these lines. They struck me with the same freshness and poignancy with which I now fancy they must have struck Descartes's contemporaries. There was about them, too, a classic ring, a splendid economy of utterance and a compelling directness of argument. The total impact was overwhelming; I was completely convinced. And I still remember the trenchant summary which I devised for myself or purloined from some forgotten source: "Our sensations bear no more resemblance to their outer causes than a feeling of pain bears to the sword that inflicts a wound."

I still know of no bolder statement of the argument. Subsequent repetitions and the burgeoning of natural science have resulted in various refinements. But they were refinements only, adding not a major stroke to the classic sketch of Descartes.

The argument itself is familiar to all. The brain, it holds in effect, is the seat of consciousness, the central switchboard of the nervous system where the myriad nerve fibers converge and to which they transmit the disturbances set up in them at their sensory endings. Here in the brain these disturbances are deciphered and collated—by a mechanism not yet fully understood. The disturbances themselves arrive in the form of neural or electro-chemical impulses—"motions" Descartes calls them— all generically identical and all conveying identically the same "message." In spite of this sameness, however, these messages on arriving at the central exchange there "cause" (excite, arouse, stimulate) in the mind or consciousness an enormous variety of "sensations" or "impressions" (sensa, sense data, etc.), the familiar colors, sounds, odors, flavors, tactile qualities, aches, pains, itches, pleasures, and so on. These elementary sensations are all on precisely the same footing; they are all subjective constituents of mind or consciousness; and some of them are the primitive materials from which, and out of which, mind then proceeds to perform its characteristic operations of perceiving and experiencing.

The differences between this argument and Galileo's argument are apparent. Descartes is not arguing *for* the distinction between primary and secondary qualities; he is arguing *from* this distinction as a premise. Nor is he arguing *for* the mathematical constitution of the world, *for* its possessing only primary qualities; he is arguing *from* this view as a premise.

Their conclusions were correspondingly different. Galileo's

conclusion is the distinction between primary and secondary qualities and the primacy of the former. Descartes's conclusion is the utter subjectivity of the secondary qualities, i.e., their status as purely mental events (sensations), and their occurrence as incorporeal effects of corporeal causes. Descartes has gone far beyond Galileo; he has removed the secondary qualities from the sense organs, from the sentient body, from the world itself. And in thus lodging them in a mind outside the natural world, in thus "subjectivizing" them, he has transformed them from secondary qualities into subjective sensations. This transformation was wrought by Descartes alone.

But this is not all that Descartes wrought. He also brought it about that the theory of sensation emerged in the guise of a "theory of ideas," as it was currently called, a theory which was even farther from Galileo's mind than the sensation theory. The theory of ideas holds in brief that *all* the direct objects of mind are nothing but its own ideas. The sensation theory holds that the direct objects of sense are but one's own sensations. The theory of ideas extends this notion from sense to all the other modes of awareness, to imagination, memory, and thought in all its forms. In this respect the theory of sensation may be regarded as a special case of the more general theory of ideas, and sensations, correspondingly, as a species of idea—the most important species, according to the British empiricists. The two theories thus arise together and flourish as virtually one.

For a reason I cannot discover, Descartes and his continental successors were strangely loathe to formulate the theory of ideas, even less the theory of sensation. For brief statements of the two theories we must turn, therefore, not to the rationalists, but to the English empiricists. In the introduction to his *Essay Concerning Human Understanding,* Locke explains that the term "idea" stands "for whatsoever is the *object* of the understanding when a man thinks . . . or whatever it is which the mind can be employed about in thinking." Berkeley is but echoing this surprising statement when he trenchantly asks: "and what do we perceive *besides our own ideas or sensations?*" (Principles, Par. 4. Berkeley's italics). Hume, as we might expect, is even more explicit, although he avoids the term "idea," this having for him a more restricted sense. It is the incontrovertible teaching of the "slightest philosophy," he contends, "that nothing can ever be present to the mind but an image or perception, and that the senses are only the inlets, through which these images are conveyed, without being able to produce any immediate intercourse between the mind and the object . . . These are the obvious dictates of reason; and no man, who reflects, ever doubted that the existences, which we consider, when we say, *this house* and *that tree,* are nothing but perceptions in the mind . . . fleeting copies or representations" (*Enquiry Concerning Human Understanding, Section XII, Part I*).

It is interesting in passing to observe that Descartes's argument for sensations has become for Hume a matter of the "slightest philosophy" involving only the "trite topics, employed by the sceptics in all ages, against the evidence of *sense*" (ibid.). For all their triteness, however, and the slightness of the philosophy which they involve, they are nonetheless incontrovertible arguments against the senses, which "no man, who reflects, ever doubted."

Such is the conclusion of Descartes's argument for sensations. In effect, it is a dual conclusion embracing both the theory of sensation and the theory of ideas. How remote this is from Galileo and the scientists of the age can best be seen by going back to the distinction between primary and secondary qualities. Using the distinction solely for its methodological virtue, the scientists were advancing by giant strides in acquiring objective knowledge of nature. Construing it as a philosophic theory of sensation, the philosophers, on the other hand, found themselves in a quandary: how on the subjective basis of ideas and impressions is such an objective knowledge of nature possible? What modern science was actually doing, modern philosophy was having trouble finding possible!

Turning now from the conclusion to the argument itself, there are a number of observations to be made. The first is that it is an argument. Now argument is not the normal means of establishing facts; facts are usually established by observation prior to argument. Sensations or sense impressions, however, are not observable facts and hence must be established by argument, as an inference from observable facts assumed as premises.

The second observation concerns these premises. Most of them are taken directly from experience. They assert such commonly observed facts as that we have physical bodies with sense organs, brains and nervous systems, that nerve fibers transmit motions or impulses, and that only by the normal functioning of this physical apparatus do we see things as colored, hear them as sounding, and so on. All this, I repeat, is quite empirical. But there is one premise, the most decisive of all, which is not empirical, not derived from observation. This is the premise that physical motions, neural impulses, actually *cause* such mental *effects* as impressions of sense. These effects are not observable, and it is also not observable that they are caused by (observable) disturbances in our nerve fibers. By this causal premise—or "causal theory of perception" as it is sometimes called—we have vaulted out of the observable into the unobservable and found ourselves at odds with naive experience.

But, you will demur, is not this causal premise just as empirical, in a way, as the rest? Is it not a matter of common observation that we have visual impressions only when our optic nerve is excited, auditory impressions only when our auditory nerve is excited, and so with all our sense organs? The answer is "yes"—but only on the assumption that we actually have such things as visual, auditory, and the other sense impressions. This, however, is just what we cannot assume; it is what we are trying to prove. If we stick by what is observable, all we can say is that we see when our optic nerve is excited, hear when our auditory nerve is excited, and so on. This is vastly different from saying that exciting our optic or auditory nerve *causes* visual or auditory impressions as mental *effects*. In the one instance we are talking about seeing and hearing, actually perceiving things with their primary and secondary qualities. In the other we are talking about sensations being caused in the mind or consciousness. It is empirically evident that we see and hear; it is not empirically evident that the colors we see and the sounds we hear are nothing but subjective sensation.

It is interesting to note what Descartes has done with this causal premise. To Galileo's one causal link between object and sense organ Descartes has added a second causal link between sense organ (or nerve impulse) and sensation. This first link is observable; the second is not. Descartes, however, might argue that the second link is not wholly without empirical warrant. He would invoke the similarity between sense perception and the sensations of tickling and pain, a similarity of which both he and Galileo made much. Admittedly tickling and pain are inner sensations and are usually caused by outer objects. Admittedly, too, in perceiving colors and sounds our eyes and ears are acted on by outer objects. In both instances outer objects act causally on parts of our bodies, on our sense organs or other nerve endings. But this one circumstance does not imply that tickling and pain are like color and sound, that as the former are inner effects of outer causes so too are the latter. We can assert this only if we assume that color and sound are subjective sense impressions. But, once again, this is just what is to be proved, not assumed.

The third observation is that there is a jarring incommensurability between physical cause and mental effect, and this in two respects. In the first respect we note a sameness on the side of the cause over against a great variety on the side of the effect. Neural impulses are so nearly alike for all nerve fibers that the fibers have been thought to be freely interchangeable throughout the whole nervous system—ideally, of course— without disturbing in the least its normal functioning. Thus the same nerve fiber and impulse in the optic nerve can cause a sensation of color and when transferred to the olfactory nerve can cause a sensation of odor. In spite of this sameness, neural impulses are said to cause sensations differing as widely as the myriad secondary qualities of things, a stupendous range of variation in both kind and degree. Descartes may be alluding to this remarkable circumstance when he asserts in the above passage that "we observe no such difference between the nerves as to lead us to judge that one set of them convey to the brain from the organs of the external senses anything different from another." But if so, he does not seem to regard it as anomolous that causes so uniformly alike should produce effects so enormously varied.

The second respect we have already noted in the monadic opposition between physical and mental, *res extensa* and *res cogitans*. Descartes sought to obviate this disparity by allowing mind and body to interact, to act causally on each other through the pineal gland. In bringing them thus into causal connection Descartes erroneously assumed that the direction of motion is not essential, i.e., that motion is not a vector quantity. This error in mechanics alone would have vitiated his causal premise. But still more influential was the metaphysical disparity between thought and extension, their monadic opposition. This rendered a causal connection between them inherently unthinkable.

In view of these difficulties it is not surprising that Descartes's causal premise should fall under attack. Malebranche, Spinoza,

Leibnitz, and Berkeley all assailed it vigorously, each for slightly different reasons, and rejected it outright. "Nothing," says Hume, "can be more inexplicable than the manner in which body should so operate upon mind as ever to convey an image of itself to a substance, supposed of so different, and even contrary a nature. It is a question of fact, whether the perceptions of the senses be produced by external objects, resembling them: How shall this question be determined? By experience surely; as in all other questions of a like nature. But here experience is, and must be entirely silent. The mind has never any thing present to it but the perceptions, and cannot possibly reach any experience of their connection with objects. The supposition of such a connection is, therefore, without any foundation in reasoning" (*Enquiry,* Sect. XII, Part I).

After Descartes the causal premise was dropped as a philosophic tenet. It was abandoned almost at once, and with it went the Cartesian argument for sensations, the one direct "proof" that the secondary qualities of things must be in sooth but subjective sensations in the perceiving mind. The argument, I repeat, because of its causal premise, lost its philosophic standing. But it did not lose its popular acceptance. It became known to every thoughtful and literate person; and its appeal was obvious, and lasting. Although banned from high philosophy, it was generally admitted into what Hume called the "slightest philosophy." Holding here its sway, as it still does, Descartes's argument was covertly accepted even by those who overtly denied its validity.

It is not surprising, then, that for all its ostensive rejection the argument for sensations should persist and its conclusion become the more secure. One would think that in impugning the argument for sensations, the theory of sensation would lose its hold. It did not. It flourished under the aegis of the new theory of ideas. Under this aegis it lost entirely its sense of being a theory, an inference from premises, a conclusion from argument. It became instead a "fundamental assumption," an axiom manifest to the "slightest philosophy." Even for Hume, and in spite of his searching scepticism, it is simply beyond doubt that the mind has never anything present to it but its own impressions and ideas.

But Hume had one luminous moment on this score, which occurred in the *Enquiry* at the close of his survey of the irreconcilable conflict between experience and reasoning. When they are experiencing, "men are carried, by a natural instinct or prepossession, to repose faith in their senses," that is, "they always suppose the very images, presented by the senses, to be the external objects, and never entertain any suspicion, that the one are nothing but representations of the other. . . . But this universal and primary opinion of all men is soon destroyed by the slightest philosophy, which teaches us, that nothing can ever be presented to the mind but an image or perception. . . . Thus the first philosophical objection to the evidence of sense or to the opinion of external existence consists in this, that such an opinion, if rested on natural instinct, is contrary to reason, and if referred to reason, is contrary to natural instinct, and at the same time carries no rational evidence with it, to convince an impartial enquirer. The second objection goes farther, and represents this opinion as contrary to reason: *at least, if it be a principle of reason, that all sensible qualities are in the mind, not in the object"* (ibid.).

The italics are mine, but the insight is Hume's. It would be Hume who thus probed to the core of the matter: *"If* it be a principle of reason that all sensible qualities are in the mind, not in the object!" I cannot but wonder what the subsequent course of philosophy might have been had Hume explored this "if" as he explored so many other alleged "principles of reason." Most of these principles turned out to be groundless pretensions, especially when they pertained to matters of fact and existence; only in mathematics, which deals with the "relations of ideas," is reason to be followed; elsewhere it should be but the slave of passion. But it is a question of fact and existence whether the sensible qualities of things are in the mind or the object; hence it is presumably beyond the province of reason. Why then does Hume in this one instance grant to reason a competence which he denies it in all similar instances? Whatever the answer, Hume unfortunately stopped at the threshold of an "enquiry" which might well have revolutionized modern philosophy.

As it was, he remained fettered to the theory of ideas and sensations. Kant, conceivably, might have loosed these fetters when, as he himself remarked, he was aroused by Hume from his dogmatic slumbers. But to what did Hume awaken him? To the theory of ideas and sensations! Kant's awakening was a fettering more complete than Hume's. What had been for Hume a matter of some question—slight, to be sure—became for Kant the dogmatic foundation of the "critical" philosophy. In laying this new foundation Kant likened it to the Copernican revolution in astronomy. "Hitherto men had assumed that all our knowledge must conform to objects; we shall now assume that objects must conform to our knowledge" (*K.d.r.V.,* B XVI). This assumption, moreover, "will be proved, not hypothetically, but apodictically" in the body of the *Critique of Pure Reason,* presumably as Copernicus in his great book "proved" his hypothesis (*K.d.r.V.,* B XXII n.).

The whole sense of this "Copernican revolution" is, of course, that the direct objects of mind are nothing but its own ideas or *Vorstellungen.* Of course, too, this "assumption" or theory is not "proved" in the body of the *Critique*; as with Hume it was simply taken for granted, a "fundamental assumption." On one important occasion, where Kant refers to this fundamental assumption, he mentions it most casually. "In such wise," he says by way of summary (A 158, B 197), "are synthetic judgments a priori possible, if we refer the formal conditions of intuition a priori, the synthesis of imagination, and the necessary unity of this latter in a transcendental apperception, to a possible experiential knowledge in general and say [or assert, *sagen*]: the conditions of the *possibility of experience* in general are at the same time the conditions of the *possibility of the objects of experience* and have thereby objective validity in a synthetic judgment a priori." The italics are Kant's and are plainly intended to point up the two members of an equation which to him is all-important. The equation is that of "experience" and "object of experience." They are the same, of course, only to the extent that they are both "ideas" or *Vorstellungen*. Only to the extent that they are thus the same can we "say" that the "conditions of the possibility" underlying the one are the same as those underlying the other.

In a philosophy which vaunts itself on being "critical" it is remarkable that a principle so foundational should require only to be "said." Nowhere is it proved or even elucidated, let alone questioned. It is beyond "criticism." It needs only the barest mention; obviously because it is self-evident, one of Whitehead's "fundamental assumptions."

It is appropriate at this juncture to take note of the inherent ambiguity in the term "idea." It stands for both experience and object, or perception and object, and may be conveniently used to signify either or both. I shall have more to say of this later. Here I wish merely to note the ambiguity of "idea" and that it rejects, by implication at least, the common-sense distinction between awareness and object. This distinction, presumably a naive product of "natural instinct or prepossession," conceals from the vulgar—as Berkely might have put it—the more learned doctrine that as "ideas" awareness and object are the same, a doctrine taught by the "slightest philosophy," that is, the theory of sensation and ideas!

Such was Descartes's argument for sensations. The argument

itself, because of its causal premise, lost its philosophic standing, although not its secret appeal. The conclusion of the argument, on the other hand, lost nothing; rather it gained in standing and swept the field. It became a "fundamental assumption" of modern philosophy, where, in the notions of "sensation" and "idea," it enjoyed an acceptance as complete as that accorded any other doctrine in the history of western thought.

But if the opinion prevailed that the sensation-idea doctrine required no support beyond itself, still the need was occasionally felt to say something in defense of the strange thesis that the secondary qualities of things are but subjective impressions in the mind. Naturally Descartes was the first to recognize this need. He responded to it with the causal argument which we have just been considering, the only direct argument I know of. He gave us also an indirect argument which we have not yet considered. After Descartes, however, the need was no longer felt on the continent; only the British empiricists seem to have recognized it, perhaps because they have never felt quite as comfortable in defying common sense as the continental rationalists. Of these, Berkeley was the most responsive. He offered an indirect argument for sensations, indirect because the direct argument was unacceptable to him, as we noted above.

To these indirect arguments for sensations I shall now turn. Because they are indirect, they will be found to lack, as one might expect, the force and vigor of the direct argument—the one argument that will prevail, covertly if not overtly, as long as the belief in sensations persists.

IV

The Indirect Arguments
for Sensations

1. Berkeley

In treating the indirect arguments for sensations I shall begin
with the British empiricists and then move back to Descartes.
The British arguments can be dealt with more briefly; and I
wish to spend more time with Descartes because of his influence
on Husserl and Phenomenology.

The British arguments are basically two in number, the one
more articulate than the other. The less articulate argument
was diffused in the new intellectual atmosphere and did not require to be brought to utterance. The new atmosphere is that
of the sensation theory. Hume referred to it, typically, as a
matter of the "slightest philosophy," as trite as the complaints
which in all ages have been raised against the senses. Everybody knows how dependent we are on our sense organs, how
they vary from person to person, even from time to time with
the same person. Everybody knows how all things sensory are
thus "relative," hence "subjective," and that this subjectivity
roots in our "sense impressions." Plainly, the direct argument

45

has done its work; it has nailed sensations firmly to the framework of modern thought and even infused them into some of our most familiar locutions.

What makes this atmosphere an indirect argument for sensations is the tendency to regard "relative" and "subjective" as though they were equivalent. This equivalence is distinctively "modern"; it did not obtain prior to Descartes. Although the relativity of the senses was well known before Descartes, it was only after him that this relativity came to signify also subjectivity. Thus to show that hot and cold are relative was for Locke tantamount to showing that they must be subjective impressions of sense, or "ideas of sensation," as he called them. Similarly, when Berkeley showed that primary qualities are equally "relative" with the secondary, it was evident at once that they must also be equally "subjective," i.e., mere ideas of sensation—or impressions of sense.* Brought to utterance, then, the indirect argument involved here is simply this: the relativity of sensory qualities is *prima facie* evidence of their subjectivity as impressions of sense.

As an argument this is quite untenable; there is no such connection between relative and subjective as is here assumed. The inference from the relativity of sense qualities to their subjectivity as sensations is possible only on the prior assumption of sensations. But in this event the argument is no longer an argument for sensations. It is no argument at all; it is but a philosophic predilection; and such indeed it was.

The more articulate argument is best set forth perhaps by George Berkeley. In the first of his *Three Dialogues between Hylas and Philonous* Berkeley argues, much like Locke before him, that "the most vehement and intense degree of heat [is] a

---

*It was only the word "idea" that made it possible to avoid the embarrassment of having to speak, and think, of primary sensations or impressions as well as secondary!

very great pain."* But, he goes on, if heat of this intensity is a subjective sensation, then heat of every intensity must also be a subjective sensation. Similarly with every sensible quality; as "immediately perceived" or felt it must be but a sense impression in the perceiving consciousness—an impression, moreover, which is indistinguishable from the pain or pleasure which it is commonly said to "cause."

The pivot of this argument is plainly the identity of heat and pain. This identity is admittedly a conclusion drawn from premises. "Seeing therefore they are both immediately perceived at the same time, and the fire affects you only with one simple, or uncompounded idea, it follows that this same simple idea is both the intense heat immediately perceived, and the pain; and consequently, that the intense heat immediately perceived, is nothing distinct from a particular sort of pain" (p. 176).

There are two premises here. The first is that "the fire affects you only with one simple, or uncompounded idea." In saying, "the fire affects you," Berkeley would seem to be reviving the discredited causal theory of perception. This he would disclaim, however, insisting that the locution was only a concession to common usage, an instance of "speaking with the vulgar." The fire itself and its affecting us are not "immediately perceived." They are "inferences." And the senses "make no inferences" (p. 174). Leaving this aside, then, let us go on to the remainder of the statement, that we are affected "only with one simple, or uncompounded, idea" when we experience the fire and its heat. In this premise Berkeley is invoking the doctrine of simple and complex ideas, which he shared with both Locke and Hume, a doctrine sometimes referred to as "psychological atomism." Remember, all "ideas of sensation" are simple. The conclusion

*P. 176. References to the *Three Dialogues* will be given by the page number of the *Works of George Berkeley, Bishop of Cloyne*, edited by A. A. Luce and T. E. Jessop, Thomas Nelson and Sons, Ltd., London, New York, 1948-57, Vol. 2.

is evident; there being but one simple idea involved, which is admittedly a subjective idea of pain, this same idea must also be the heat which we "immediately perceive." Therefore, heat and all secondary qualities must be subjective "ideas of sensation," or more briefly, "sensations."

The second premise is not openly stated. It lies implicit in the term "idea" and hence underlies the first premise. We have already noted that by "idea" Berkeley means what we "immediately perceive," and what we "immediately perceive" is nothing but our own ideas or sensations. Notice in the above brief quotation that he uses "immediately perceived" three times. This is obviously his principal premise: not that the fire affects us with one simple idea, but rather that the heat and the pain "are both immediately perceived." For to be immediately perceived is to be forthwith a subjective idea of sensation. This is the bare bones of Berkeley's argument. It is superfluous to say that the heat is perceived at the same time as the pain, that the two are but one simple idea; it only obscures the fact that the argument is a *petitio principii,* that it has covertly assumed what it would ostensibly prove—sensations.

2. *Descartes*

Descartes's indirect argument for sensations is quite different from those of the English empiricists. It is characteristically more elaborate. Its general purport is that since experience *may* be but a consistent dream or hallucination, it *must* be a process of the same ilk operating on sensory materials of the same kind, namely, subjective sensations. As an argument for sensations it too will turn out to prove only what it has already assumed— sensations. Let us now follow this classic argument in the *Meditations* of Descartes.

Consider, says Descartes, the phenomena of dreams, the delusions of madness and delirium, hallucinations, and the like, and reflect on the power and vividness with which they frequently occur. "Dwelling carefully on this reflection," he continues, "I see so manifestly that there are no certain indications by which we may clearly distinguish wakefulness from sleep that I am lost in astonishment. And my astonishment is such that it is almost capable of persuading me that I now dream" (*Meditation I*). The pivot of this argument is "that there are no certain indications by which we may clearly distinguish wakefulness from sleep," whence it is "manifestly" possible that they are not actually distinct at all, but that experience is a kind of dream (or hallucination) and the world a grandiose illusion.

Descartes, it may be well to note, does not assume, let alone prove, that experience *is* a dream: nor does he believe it for a minute. And he does not deny the existence of an external world; he proves this in the sixth *Meditation*. His concern at this juncture is merely to avoid accepting for "certain" or "indubitable" anything which he finds subject to a "possible doubt." The fact that experience *may* be a dream, hence that the world *may* not exist, plainly renders these matters subject to a possible doubt and warrants laying them aside for the time being *as though* they were false. Descartes is content, therefore, with the bare possibility that experience *may* be a kind of dream or hallucination, and that the world *may* not exist.

This bare possibility, however, that experience may be a dream, speaks volumes. Notice its onesidedness: experience may be a kind of dream, not dream a kind of experience. On the sole basis that the two are not clearly distinguishable why should the one be said to be a version of the other, not the other a version of the one? The answer, I think, can easily be surmised. It is clear to Descartes that dreaming and hallucinating are fabricating or constituting modes of awareness, not discovering modes—to use my own terms, not Descartes's. It is *not* clear to Descartes

that experience and perception are discovering modes of awareness. All that is clear to him about experience and perception
is that they possess a sensory content, the same content we
find in dreams and hallucinations. And since this content is
patently subjective in the one instance, it must also be subjective in the other. The conclusion is unavoidable: experience
must be a kind of dream, not dream a kind of experience, because the content is subjective sensations.

3. External Experience As Operation and Idea

But if experience is *possibly* a kind of dream or hallucination,
must it not be *actually* a constituting or fabricating mode of
awareness? For if it were *actually* a discovering mode of awareness, it could not possibly be a constituting mode and hence not
even possibly a kind of dream or hallucination. Experience, in
short, can *possibly* be a kind of dream or hallucination only if
experience is *actually* a constituting, not a discovering, mode of
awareness.

The question now boils down to what external experience
and perception *actually are*. Either they are discovering modes
of awareness or fabricating modes of awareness. For the natural
attitude they are discovering modes, not fabricating (or constituting), and discovery is their intrinsic mark just as fabrication
is the intrinsic mark of dreams and hallucinations. By virtue of
these criteria the two modes of awareness are so clearly distinct
that neither one can be said to be even possibly a version of
the other.

But if this is evident to the natural attitude of common sense,
it was not evident to Descartes. To him the contrary was evident;
there are no distinguishing marks. "I see so manifestly that there
are no certain indications by which we may clearly distinguish
wakefulness from sleep that I am lost in astonishment." Before

giving way to astonishment, however, notice that what is here manifest to Descartes is 1) the *absence* of distinguishing marks on the side of perception and experience, and 2) the *presence* of distinguishing marks on the side of dreams, delusions and hallucinations. The presence of these latter marks is revealed in the fact that Descartes has not the slightest doubt about the fabricating or constituting nature of dreams and hallucinations. Only the nature of sense perception and experience is not manifest.

This is a curious disparity, because both perceiving and dreaming are operations of consciousness, *cogitationes,* and fall equally within the purview of the indubitable certainty which I have of myself as a thinking being, or *res cogitans.* Among the operations, or *cogitationes,* which constitute my nature as a *res cogitans* Descartes repeatedly mentions perception (which he does not distinguish from experience), adding that "although the things which I perceive and imagine are perhaps nothing at all apart from me and in themselves, I am nevertheless assured that these modes of thought (*cogitationes*) which I call perceptions and imaginations, inasmuch only as they are modes of thought, certainly reside and are met with in me" (*Med.* III and passim.). That this holds for *all* the operations of consciousness is explicitly stated; "by the word 'thought' (*cogitatio*) I understand all that of which we are conscious as operating within us" (*Principles,* IX). Manifestly, then, perception (experience) and imagination, being operations of consciousness, are matters of indubitable certainty, possessing intrinsic marks by which they can be clearly distinguished both from each other and from all other *cogitationes* of consciousness. The nature of sense perception and imagination must be as manifest as the nature of dreams and hallucinations.

Descartes is here plainly at odds with himself. The trouble is the theory of sensation and ideas. For if the "adventitious ideas" of perception are but subjective sensations, then perception and experience do indeed have the same sensory content as dreams and hallucinations. This, however, is just what is to be proved, not assumed. Descartes assumed it nonetheless, and in so doing he quietly overlooked the certain indications by which we can —and actually do—distinguish between outer perception and dreams. In removing these indications Descartes also misconstrued the nature of outer perception and misassessed the quality of its evidence. Let us take a closer look at experience and its evidence.

In turning to external experience it may be well to remind ourselves at the outset of one obvious point. Both external experience and its warrant, the quality of its evidence, are "objects" only for internal experience, i.e., introspection or reflection. As an object of internal experience, external experience is a mode of awareness, an operation of consciousness, a *cogitatio,* clearly distinct both from its (outer) object and from all other (inner) operations of consciousness. Similarly, its warrant, the evidential quality of its disclosures, is an object for reflection alone, an object moreover inseparable from external experience itself.

Reflecting on this warrant we call to mind the familiar complaints which in all ages have been raised against the senses. Sense experience, they say, is quite unreliable; its warrant is hopelessly prejudiced by the fallibility of its constituent perceptions. Now sense perceptions are undeniably fallible; they abound in errors, distortions, illusions. This is an incontrovertible fact. But on whose authority? Is it not experience itself which shows up these errors of sense; and does it not expose these errors in the very process of correcting them? Consider for a minute this inherent power of self-correction.

It is exercised in every waking instant, in every one of the myriad adjustments, accommodations we are constantly making and have to make because perception confronts us only with the perspectives of things. Every object we perceive is beheld at a given distance, from a certain angle, under these or those conditions of visibility, audibility, and so on. Never do we perceive an object otherwise than through these perspectival appearances. It is to these that we adjust in perceiving the things thus appearing. Without this adjustment we should be quite deceived, sooner or later fatally deceived. As adults we have learned to allow for most of these perspectives almost without thinking. A few however are so striking that we have to discount them more or less thinkingly as "illusions," optical illusions like the wet spot on the road ahead, the converging of the railroad tracks, the oar bent in water, mirages, and the like. There are also auditory and tactual illusions, such as echos, the Doppler effect, and others. In precisely the same way we discern and allow for fancies, dreams, and more rarely hallucinations. If at times we are "taken in" by these illusory appearances, or apparitions, still it is the normal course of experience to expose these errors in the process of correcting them. And external experience is "normal" only to the extent that it is thus self-correcting.

In this power of self-correction lies the warrant of external experience. By this power experience redeems itself, so to speak, from the errors of sense. By this power, which exposes as it corrects, experience neutralizes without extinguishing the fallibility of perception and acquires thereby that *authenticity* which it has for us all as we live it from cradle to grave. This is not to say that experience is thus rendered infallible. But it is to say that experience is not so utterly fallible as to be a possible tissue of illusions—a grand hallucination.

Being neither infallible nor yet merely fallible, the warrant of external experience lies somewhere in between. Were experience infallible its deliverances would be beyond doubt, indubitable; their denial would involve us in inconsistency if not outright contradiction; they would be *apodictic*. Were it on the other hand merely fallible, its deliverances would be utterly dubious, indecisive, admitting equally of affirmation or denial, in a word *problematic.* Between these two lies what has been called *assertoric;* the deliverances of external experience are assertoric in quality, that is, they give rise to assertions of "fact." These assertions of fact are unlike apodictic statements in that they can be denied without contradiction and hence are ever open to future confirmation and correction. They are unlike problematic statements in that their denial is contrary to fact and hence not equally possible with their affirmation. Lacking the high finality of the apodictic and the utter indecisiveness of the problematic, the assertoric evidence of external experience has its own unique force and value, that of the empirical "facts" of life and science.

But if the warrant of external experience is assertoric, that of isolated perceptions is not; it is merely problematic. An isolated perception, ripped from the fabric of experience, with its connections severed and its edges so frayed that we cannot tell where it begins or ends, such a perception like a mounted specimen can yield only an inert evidence, wholly inconclusive, problematic. Whether this evidence is to be affirmed or denied, in whole or in part, no one can possibly say. Only subsequent perceptions can decide this. But no subsequent perception, similarly excised, is in a position to do the deciding. For the same disability attaches to every subsequent perception as attaches to the given perception; each is so utterly problematic as to require confirmation before it can confirm. Hence no isolated perception can possibly confirm another; confirmation is not only a prospect indefinitely deferred; it is an impossibility in principle. In other words, no sum of problematic evidences can yield an assertoric evidence; the two are as different from each other as from apodictic evidence.

What is amiss here is patently the artificial isolation. Abandon this artifice, restore perceptions to the living fabric of experience, allow them to function normally in its authenticating process, and the whole picture clears up at once. No longer merely fallible and requiring a validation that can never come off, perceptions are now by virtue of this living context both validating, and validated, the springs of assertoric evidence. Such is the authenticity of external experience, its assertoric warrant.

Assertoric *evidence* has as a companion piece assertoric *certainty*. Most of the certainties we live by are of this quality. Consider but one of them, one of the most important of all, the living certainty we all have of the existence of the sensible world in which we are born and live and die. I call this a living certainty because it is so nearly one with human life that without it our mortal existence would be unimaginable. Notice too how impregnable it is to all assaults of theory. Challenge, even deride it as one will, its imperious hold remains unshaken in the all-important business of living. We cannot live without it; we can only philosophize without it.

This certainty, being assertoric, not apodictic, does not leave open as a genuine possibility that the sensible world does not exist. This possibility is not a "real" possibility, it is only a "logical" possibility, i.e., it can be thought without contradiction. To regard this empty, merely logical possibility (that the world does not exist) as of equal weight with the assertoric actuality (that the world does in fact exist) is to deny altogether the assertoric and to reduce the assertoric to the status of the problematic. This is what Descartes did when he admitted only two kinds of evidence, apodictic and problematic.

Descartes was moved to this view of evidence by his mathematical predilection for "clear and distinct ideas." Mathematical "ideas" (objects?) are clear and distinct; their evidence is apodictic and yields indubitable certainty. All other evidence, being unclear and indistinct, is merely problematic and cannot yield true certainty. The evidence of inner experience Descartes found to be apodictic like that of mathematical "ideas." The evidence of outer experience he found to be not apodictic, hence merely problematic and totally unfit for the secure founding of philosophy. No mention of assertoric evidence or assertoric certainty.

Descartes's penchant for the apodictic and his consequent neglect of the assertoric were widely shared in the ensuing development of modern philosophy. Even today and in spite of much professed empiricism the inclination is to regard but one certainty as worthy of the name, a certainty that will brook no doubt. Rarely is certainty construed otherwise than as apodictic or indubitable. In philosophic discussions the usual test is: Are you absolutely sure? Are your criteria "adequate"? Can your statement be denied without contradiction? If it can be so denied, it is not genuinely certain and cannot be acceptable to reason; it is merely problematic—as though there were no such thing as assertoric evidence and certainty, or as though they were not philosophically respectable.

The scientific tradition was not as adamant in its preference for the apodictic. For a while this preference did prevail and was quite exclusive. It reached its apogee, perhaps, in Laplace's famous "ideal" of mechanical determinism. But this ideal was admittedly one which only an "infinite intellect" could possibly realize. From here on it began to recede. With the advent of relativity, quantum theory, and the indeterminacy principle it was finally superseded by "probability." In probability the classical notion of the assertoric has returned under a new name and under new auspices and is rapidly regaining its respectability.

But Descartes had a second reason for overlooking the assertoric. Besides his mathematical penchant for the formal and apodictic he had also a firm commitment to the theory of sensation. According to this theory sense perception is in effect nothing but the having and manipulating of our own sensations or "ideas." It follows from this that sense perception cannot possibly reveal to us anything about an existence other than its own. We may "infer" or "posit" such an other and outer existence on the basis of what we thus perceive within; but this inference has no immediate warrant in perception itself, and the senses do not infer. Perception itself, being an "idea" and as such both object and awareness, can bear witness only to itself as an operation or "content of consciousness." In this respect it is apodictically evident—as an object of introspection. In every other respect it is problematic. Should it correspond perchance to an object outside the mind this correspondence would be for the idea something wholly adventitious and for the mind unknowable.

Whether for these two reasons or not, Descartes recognized only two kinds of evidence, apodictic and problematic, thus virtually denying the assertoric. In denying the assertoric he reduced the evidence of sense experience to the level of the problematic and construed the empirical evidence of the world's existence as a mere possibility no greater than the possibility of the world's nonexistence. Only by thus depriving sense experience of its assertoric warrant could Descartes hold as equally and "really" possible 1) that the world does not exist and 2) that the world does exist.

4. Internal Experience

Fortunately the theory of sensation did not similarly threaten internal experience and its apodictic warrant. Descartes saw clearly that on turning inward our attention falls on "objects" which are immediately present and evident beyond doubt. These inner objects are the acts and contents of our "stream of consciousness"—an expression which Descartes did not use. He saw, too, that these acts are grasped apodictically as *cogitationes,* that is, as individual instances of general operations, the "operations of consciousness." This conjunction of particularity and universality in inner perception is worthy of some comment.

Ask anybody who seems to be lost in thought what he is thinking about and he will invariably reply, "I was looking at the carving on that table," or "I was listening to the music next door," or, "I was imagining what it would be like to be in Mexico," or, "I was thinking about my income tax." And so on. In every instance his report will contain some such general term as "looking," "listening," "imagining," "thinking," each of which signifies not an individual act, but a *kind* of activity, a general operation,—or *cogitatio,* as Descartes called it. Obviously, such a "kind" cannot possibly occur; it is not an individual event in time, but a timeless generality under which individual events may fall as "instances." To report merely that I was looking, therefore, would convey only the general nature of what I was doing. There are myriad acts of looking. Only when I add, "looking at the carving on that table," do I begin to convey something of the individuality of the unique act I was actually performing. Even so, the report falls short of conveying the full individuality of the act. No report can do this; the most it can do is describe certain general features of the act in such detail as will suffice for the purpose in hand. In nearly every instance the first of these general features is the kind or species of the act, the operation of which it is an instance; the second is the object of the act, the "content" of the act as it is often unfelicitously called.

I am quite aware that the term "act of consciousness" is not in good odor. But I see no convenient way of avoiding it, or any advantage in doing so. My conscious life, if seems to me, is an "activity" in which I perform countless "acts." These acts are all individual and unique and vary greatly in complexity, some containing others as parts. This suggests that there may be acts so utterly simple that like atoms they possess no distinguishable parts at all. If there are such atomic acts, I have not been able to discover them. All acts, I find, are complex, to the extent, at least, of having distinguishable parts, as we shall see more fully later on. Acts can combine to form more complex acts, and these in turn still higher acts, and so on up to the stream of consciousness itself. In a way the whole life of an individual may be said to be one act. This entails that no act can be isolated except in thought, and that every act, embedded as it is in the stream of consciousness, merges at both ends into other acts and above into higher acts. Below, it may have simpler acts as constituent parts. "Act" in short is an indefinite term, even arbitrary, like the term "object." But it is not for this reason useless. No other term, I believe, signifies quite as poignantly what is going on inside us, so far at least as this inner activity is an articulated process with discernible segments.

Turning, then, to the acts which were reported above, my point is that these acts, and all acts, can be grasped and expressed only as individual instances of general operations, *cogitationes*. In every instance an act of which I am aware is grasped as an act of seeing or hearing or touching, of remembering, imagining, thinking, judging, feeling, willing, or the like, always as an individual instance of an "operation," or kind of activity. Were this not so my inner gaze would be but a mute awareness—if, indeed, an awareness at all—of my flowing stream of consciousness with its constant coming and going of nameless events, some together, others overlapping, most in sequence. To this inert gaze each event for the duration of its occurrence would be present or "now," actual only this once. Once over and done with, it would vanish into an oblivion beyond recall. In this event introspection would be as shifting as the stream it contemplates, a fleeting and ineffable awareness hardly worthy of the name.

Plainly this is not what introspection grasps. What it grasps is not a mere Heraclitean flux, but an articulated process with discernible segments, each an instance of a timeless operation. If this circumstance is not a mere accident of language, nor a feature imposed on the stream by introspection itself, then it must lie in the nature of consciousness that its acts actually embody operations. And since these operations are actually embodied or incorporated, they are not "classes" but real "species" or "essences." For individuals do not instance or embody classes; they are only members of classes, of numberless classes at that, whereas each act embodies but a single essence.

Be this as it may, it is only as instances of operations that we grasp acts in introspection, identify them for what they are, bring them to utterance, and repeat them in essence, i.e., *in specie,* not *individualiter,* and make them "objects" of philosophic reflection.

This conjunction or union of particular and universal, of act and operation, of instance and essence, is more widely recognized than one might at first assume. I have already adduced common usage in reporting what goes on within us. Empirical psychology, even when it eschews the language and evidence of introspection, is still preoccupied with operations or processes— the "learning process" for example. Curiously, this operational grasp is nowhere more conspicuous than in mathematics. An arithmetic operation—addition, for example—is not a psychological act or event in time. It may be exemplified by psychological acts in time, any number of them, as when we actually add a column of figures. But addition itself as a mathematical operation can never thus occur. It is a timeless entity possessing only such properties as commutation, association, and the like. Psychological acts of addition, on the other hand, are not timeless entities, but actual events in time, each and all exemplifying or instancing the one operation of addition. Similarly with every other operation in mathematics. It is not surprising, then, that

Descartes the mathematician should view the acts of consciousness as operations, or *cogitationes,* and should take them in this
respect as apodictically evident. That individual acts, too, may
be apodictically evident to introspection he neither affirms nor
denies. He is interested in acts only in their essential character
as operations and the apodictic certainty with which they can be
grasped. Even his interest in them as operations, however, did
not extend much beyond their being items in the primal certainty
which I have of myself as a *res cogitans.* Hence he was content
in the main simply to list them in his several inventories (all
of them partial) of the *cogitationes* of consciousness.

In each of these inventories he lists external experience or
sense perception (*sentire, sensus*) and distinguishes it without
further ado from imagining, thinking, willing, and presumably
from all the other operations of consciousness, including dreams,
delusions, and hallucinations. This can only mean that there
are in fact "certain indications" by which we can "clearly distinguish" external experience from dreams and hallucinations,
that these indications are indubitably clear and distinct, and that
they delineate external experience as a discovering mode of
awareness yielding assertoric evidence.

All of this follows on Descartes's own showing and refutes,
once again, his argument that because it lacks intrinsic marks
external experience may be a kind of dream or hallucination.
Since it has intrinsic marks apodictically evident to reflection,
external experience cannot possibly be a kind of dream or hallucination. But if it is impossible that experience should be a
dream or hallucination, is it still possible that the world does
not exist, that it is an illusion? By the assertoric warrant of experience the existence of the world is an empirical fact. The
possibility that the world does not exist is therefore contrary to
fact, not a "real" possibility. It is nonetheless logical, since the
evidence of experience is not *apodictic.* As such it is quite empty

and quite unfit to serve as a premise in a serious philosophic argument, especially when there is an appeal to empirical fact.

This is not Descartes's view because, as we noted in the preceding section, he construed the warrant of experience as problematic—as the sensation theory would seem to entail—and so could regard as equally real 1) the possibility that the world does not exist, that it is an illusion, and 2) the possibility that the world does exist, that it is not an illusion. Inasmuch as Descartes bequeathed this view, along with the sensation theory, to a number of his successors, Husserl among them, it is fitting that we take a closer look at the view and at some of its consequences.

5. Possible and Contingent Existence

Assuming with Descartes that the two possibilities are equally real, we must then regard them as suspended in a kind of balance in which neither possibility outweighs the other. For if either one were to outweigh the other, the balance would be destroyed, the preponderant member would be not merely possible, but actual or necessary, and the outweighed member would be no longer possible (in the initial sense), but contrary to fact or impossible. In order for either side to be possible in this "problematic" sense, both sides must be equally possible; they must form a balanced pair. Only then is the situation strictly problematic.

Taking now the balanced pair, the possibility that the world exists and the possibility that the world does not exist, we may then compress this pair into the single statement that the existence of the world is not necessary. For if the existence of the world were necessary there would be no possibility that it does not exist; and if there were no possibility that the world does not exist, there would be no balancing possibility that it does exist, its existence would be actual or necessary, not possible. Both possibilities vanish if the world exists necessarily; they obtain only if the world does not exist necessarily. Hence the balance of possibilities can be boiled down to the statement that the existence of the world is not necessary.

This statement, however, may be construed in two very different ways. So far we have construed it as signifying the possibility-pair that the world may exist or not exist; so far nothing more. But there is another way of construing it and that is to take it as implying the classical doctrine of "contingency," which also holds that the existence of the world is not necessary. This contingency doctrine, however, has nothing to do with our possibility doctrine; and to assume that it does is to fall into a serious confusion. It is imperative that the two doctrines be held carefully apart.

The classical doctrine of contingency holds that the world does not exist "necessarily" but only "contingently," that its contents are not "necessary beings" but "contingent beings." They are said to be contingent because their essence does not involve existence. A moment's reflection will make this clear. Existence is involved in our *perception* of things; since, as the natural attitude holds, we can perceive only what is "there" (existent) to be perceived. But conception is not thus limited by existence; we can think and talk of what is nonexistent as well as of what exists, of things that no longer exist or do not yet exist or cannot exist at all. The reason for this is that in merely conceiving things—as distinct from perceiving them—what we grasp of them is their nature or essence, "what" they are. Of this nature or essence existence is not a part; it is not a "real predicate," as Kant put it; for it adds nothing one way or the other to "what" a thing is. In this respect all things are equally capable of existing or not existing. If they do exist, therefore, their existence must derive from something other than their essence, something that must be already existing, since existence can come only from existence, not from essence. Now if this other existing thing is similarly capable of not existing, then its existence must in turn derive from yet a third existing thing. And so on without end so long as we are dealing with things whose existence is derived or "contingent."

All things temporal are in this sense contingent and so is the whole order and assemblage of things in time, the world. There would be no difficulty here were it not for the fact that this contingent existence is also *actual*. We are assured of this actuality by the assertoric witness of experience. Being actual this contingent existence can be adequately accounted for only by assuming a "sufficient reason or ground," namely, another existence, not contingent, not capable of not existing, but "neces-sary"—a thing, in other words, which exists necessarily because its essence precludes the possibility of nonexistence; or, what is the same thing, whose essence involves or includes existence.

Descartes's version of this argument is somewhat different though not conflicting. Instead of focusing on the essence of things existing in time, he focuses instead on the nature of tem-poral existence itself, more precisely on the order of instants in the duration of anything existing in time. In the successive course of its existence, no matter how long or short its duration, a thing actually exists at only one instant at a time, never at all instants at once, simultaneously or *tota simul*. Consider one such instant or "now" in the duration of a thing's existence. Existing "now" it exists no longer at past instants and not yet at future instants. Hence neither its past existence nor its future existence, since both are now nonexistent, could possibly be the sufficient cause of its present existence. Nor could anything existing simul-taneously with the thing in the same "now" cause its existence, for there is no time in the "now" to exercise this causality; all empirical causality "takes time," requires duration, and presupposes existence in time—the very thing that is here in question. There is, in short, no sufficient cause *in time* for the *existence* of anything at any instant of its duration in time. If there be such a sufficient cause for existence in time, this cause must *exist* not *seriatim* in time but *tota simul* outside or beyond time.

A corollary of this argument might be called the "hazard of existence." At any given instant in its duration the existence of a thing precludes its nonexistence for that instant. But the respite is only momentary; for the very next instant and all future instants hang in a quivering balance of being or not being which nothing in the "now," still less in the past or future, can possibly tilt. Thus even while existing a thing confronts nonexistence as an ever-present possibility, a constant threat, as it were, menacing every instant in its duration. In conscious beings this threat or hazard may arouse a kind of "existential anxiety." But this is not an explicit tenet of the classical doctrine of contingency.

Whatever you may think of this argument for contingency and for postulating a necessary existence, one thing is unmistakably clear: what is said to be contingent is not a *possible* existence but an *actual* existence, the actual existence of things in time and the world. Only actual existence can be contingent or necessary. A possible existence is so far only possible, not even contingent, let alone necessary. In holding, therefore, that the existence of the world is not necessary, the contingency doctrine takes this existence of the world as actual (assertoric), not as merely possible (problematic). Correlatively, the lurking possibility which renders this existence contingent is the (threatening) possibility of *not* existing, not the mere possibility of existing.

This understanding of the proposition, "the existence of the world is not necessary," is plainly different from our former understanding of the proposition as signifying simply the possibility-pair, the world may or may not exist. This difference should be sharpened and made verbally manifest.

This can be done simply by recalling the possibility-pair and noting how the possibility that the world does not exist is virtually one with the possibility that experience is a kind of dream or hallucination. For if experience is a dream or hallucination, then the world is an illusion and its existence is not necessary *to our experience of it*; we can experience a world whether the world exists or not. The italicized words make clear at once what is meant here by "not necessary"; it means not necessary *in relation to experience*. Of "necessary" as an intrinsic quality, opposed to "contingent," it says absolutely nothing. It completely ignores actual existence, as it ignores assertoric evidence, and hence does not even hint at the contingency doctrine. What it does assert refers primarily to the nature of experience, not existence, and it is in relation to experience alone that the existence of the world is said to be not necessary. "Not necessary" is thus an ellipsis for the phrase "not necessary to experience." On this understanding the proposition should read, "the existence of the world is not necessary to experience."

The corresponding reading for the contingency doctrine should be, "the existence of the world is not necessary in itself." The slight difference in wording makes clear at once the vast difference in meaning. It makes the word "necessary" refer in the one case to a relative property, and in the other to an intrinsic property of existence itself. It reveals at the same time that the opposite of necessary, "not necessary," is equivalent in the one case to "possible" and in the other to "contingent," two very distinct terms. Clearly the important difference here is that the one proposition—or doctrine—is principally about experience, the other about existence.

6. Experience and Existence

According to Descartes's argument the possibility that the world does not exist is a consequence of the possibility that experience may be an illusion. For if it is really possible that experience is an illusion, then plainly experience does not depend in any way on the existence of a world; it can take place without a world; the "world" in this instance would be simply the "ideas" we directly perceive. Obviously the existence of such a world is not necessary to experience. Curiously, Descartes never said this. He implied it plainly enough; but he did not say it in so many words. Some of his successors did say it, among them Husserl, and in saying it went on to equate "not necessary" with "contingent" as though the nature of existence were determined by the nature of the experience in which it is given, contingent existence in problematic experience, necessary existence in apodictic experience. Descartes was spared this confusion by holding to the classical doctrine of contingency.

According to this classical doctrine the contingency of existence does not follow from the assertoric quality of experience, nor does the assertoric quality of experience follow from the contingency of existence. The two are independent, at least to the extent that contingency and necessity are intrinsic properties of existence without regard to experience, whereas assertoric and apodictic are qualities of experience without regard to existence. Because they are thus independent Descartes could hold to the one (contingency) while abandoning the other (assertoric). Also, because they are independent they can be combined in four different ways. We can have

1) assertoric experience of contingent existence,
2) assertoric experience of necessary existence,

3) apodictic experience of contingent existence, and

4) apodictic experience of necessary existence.

If there be such a thing as experience of a necessary being, it would fall under 2) or 4), possibly both. But I set these aside in order to focus on 1) and 3), since 1) refers to our external experience of the outer world, and 3) refers to our internal experience of our inner conscious selves.

I am particularly interested in 3), since it brings out the point that apodictic experience does not entail necessary existence. Although inner experience yields apodictic evidence of consciousness and its operations, it does not make their existence necessary. Descartes was perfectly clear on this point. What is "necessary" here is not the existence of my psychic operations or acts, or—what is the same thing—my existence as a conscious (as Descartes put it, "thinking") being. What is "necessary" is solely the proposition (*pronunciatum*) which asserts this existence. This proposition, moreover, is necessary only in the sense of being "necessarily true." And it is necessarily true because the apodictic evidence on which it is based cannot, in this instance at least, be denied without contradiction. For if every act of thinking is an implicit assertion of my existence, then I cannot possibly deny my existence, since the very act of denying it would implicitly assert it and thus involve me in contradiction. What is necessary, therefore, is not my existence but only the truth of the proposition which asserts my existence.

Even this logical necessity, however, is not unqualified. It is subject to two limitations. 1) The proposition in question must be phrased solely in the first person singular: *I* must assert *my* existence. Only for me is my existence apodictically evident; only my reflections can grasp my acts with indubitable immediacy. For nobody else is my existence thus evident; and nobody else's existence is thus evident to me. Only for me in relation to myself is the evidence apodictic and the proposition undeniable.

Expressed in the second or third person the proposition loses completely its necessity; it ceases to be a necessary truth. And all because my existence is not necessary in itself, but only contingent. 2) Not only must this proposition be couched in the first person singular, it must also be restricted to the present tense. On this too Descartes was perfectly clear. "Having reflected well and carefully examined all things, we must come to the definite conclusion that this proposition: I am, I exist, is necessarily true each time that I pronounce it, or that I mentally conceive it . . . I am, I exist, this is certain. But how often? Just when I think; for it might possibly be the case if I ceased entirely to think, that I should likewise cease altogether to exist" (*Meditation II*). The proposition holds, in short, only so long as I am thinking or am actively conscious. It says nothing of my existence when I may not be thinking, say before birth or after death. Hence I *can* think of myself as not existing at times when I am not thinking, and this without a semblance of contradiction. The thought of my coming to be and passing away, the thought of my existence as contingent, is thoroughly consistent with the *cogito ergo sum* and with the apodictic evidence on which it is based.

What this all signifies is not alone that the proposition which asserts my existence is necessarily true only when uttered in the first person singular and in the present tense. It also signifies that this proposition is subject to these limitations *because my existence is contingent, not necessary*. The important thing here is that I have apodictic experience of (my own) contingent existence. This is important because it shows at once that apodictic evidence and the necessary truths to which it gives rise do not imply or entail necessary existence. This means that we cannot infer from the apodictic warrant of inner experience to the necessary existence of consciousness. There is no such connection between inner experience and its object and none between outer experience and its object. Descartes did not assume such a connection; but Husserl did, as we shall see in Chapter VII.

7. *Summary*

Descartes's indirect argument for sensations begins by assuming that sense experience possesses no intrinsic marks to distinguish it clearly from dream or hallucination. This gives rise at once to the real possibility that sense experience is a dream or hallucination and to the accompanying possibility that the world does not exist, that it is an illusion. This is tantamount to saying that the existence of the world is not necessary to experience, that as what we dream or hallucinate need not exist, so what we experience need not exist.

This view, I believe, rests on one initial assumption: the theory of sensation. Only if we first assume that the immediate objects of sense perception are sensations or ideas, can we then liken experience to a dream or hallucination and take as real the possibility that it may really be such. In this event the argument would invalidate itself by covertly assuming what it would prove; like most of the others, it would be an argument *from* sensations, not *for* sensations.

Misled by the theory of sensation Descartes took for "real" a possibility which is in fact "unreal," merely logical, empty. This involved reducing the warrant of sense experience from assertoric to problematic. Husserl followed Descartes in this and went one step farther; he construed the apodictic and assertoric warrants of inner and outer experience as definite indices of necessary and contingent existence.

We have now completed our survey of the arguments for sensations, direct and indirect, and have found them all untenable. Let us now return to the theory of sensation and ideas and follow its further development, especially that phase of its development in which the successors of Descartes attempt to show how from sensations we get experience and knowledge of an empirical world. We can see from the outset that this process will be the reverse of the subjectivizing process by which sensations were originally got—a process of "production" rather than a process of "reduction." Let us examine the principal steps in this process of "production," not so much in historical detail as rather schematically with our eyes fixed on the exigencies of the problem itself.

V
Production or Constitution

1. Sensation and Perception

The first step in the process of production is to distinguish, as had not been done before Descartes, between "sensation" and "perception," correlatively, between "sensing" and "perceiving." The reason for making this distinction is the manifest difference between inner sensations and outer sense qualities. Sensing is the original having or receiving of impressions, whereas perceiving is the beholding of these as sense qualities of objects. By the first we have only a flood of inner impressions; by the second we have before us relatively stable complexes appearing as sense objects. Sensation is clearly prior to perception in that it provides the raw materials on which perception operates. Also, sensing is a kind of passivity or receptivity, whereas perceiving is a kind of activity or spontaneity. For although sensations may have external causes, there is no external cause of their being worked over and combined into sense objects. There is, for example, no outside stimulus causing me to transform and put together the visual, auditory and tactual impressions which I allegedly receive on picking up a baby's rattle. The different kinds of sensations may be separately caused from without, but not their

72

combination; this is my own doing on perceiving the rattle as a single sense object.

Although distinct, sensation and perception rarely if ever occur separately. Perception obviously cannot occur without sensation. Sensation, on the other hand, being prior to perception, might conceivably occur without it. Actually, however, the instant we have sense impressions we find ourselves perceiving sense qualities. Rarely, if ever, do we merely sense or merely have sense impressions; invariably we perceive them as sense qualities of things. This would suggest that perceiving, even though an activity, is almost as involuntary as sensing, that we cannot help perceiving sense objects with their sense qualities any more than we can help having sensations. Sensation, we might say, automatically "triggers" perception. This means that the activity of perceiving occurs simultaneously with the passive occurrence of sensations and, like sensations, must lie beyond the reach of observation.

This simultaneity entails that there is no lapse of time between the occurrence of sensations and their appearance as sense qualities, that sensations do not linger in the raw state or in any transition state, but are transformed the instant they occur. In this respect the process of perceiving is quite unlike any empirical process with which we are familiar. For all empirical processes extend over a certain interval of time, no matter how short, in the course of which the raw materials progress through successive stages before emerging as end products. Here, however, there is no such progressive transformation, no lapse of time between raw material and end product. Sense impressions and sense qualities are simultaneous in a fashion which seems to preclude any progressive transition from one to the other. The transition, therefore, must be, if not instantaneous, yet so exceedingly swift as utterly to escape detection, perhaps of the speed of some nuclear reactions. In any event we are dealing

with unobservables—sensations, their transformation into sense
qualities, and the brief duration of this transforming process,
about which I shall have more to say later on. Because they are
unobservable we can only frame hypotheses about them based
on our observation of the end products. Let us proceed with
these hypotheses.

2. Perception and Imagination

The first hypothesis is that what we call perception is really
the work of the imagination and that this work advances in
several stages. The first and lowest stage would be that of transforming sense impressions into sense qualities. A second and
higher stage, or stages, would be that of "combining," or "asso-
ciating," or "synthesizing" these sense qualities into the sense
complexes which we call sense objects, and these in turn into a
sensory world. This complication of stages should not surprise
us when we reflect that the total process we are considering is
nothing less than that of fashioning for ourselves perceptions—
more, a whole lifelong experience—of sense objects in a sensible
world. This is truly an immense performance. Kant was perhaps
the first to comprehend its magnitude and to probe its hidden
intricacies in his monumental *Critique of Pure Reason*. For all
its complexity, however, the process had for Kant one principal
dynamic agency: the human imagination, which he described as
"an art (*Kunst*) hidden in the depths of the human soul whose
true processes (*Handgriffe*) we shall hardly ever extract from
nature and bring unveiled to view" (*K.d.r.V.*, A 141, B 181).

Obviously, this imagining which is one with perceiving is
sharply to be distinguished from imagination in the usual sense of
the term. Usually in the natural attitude we are at pains to hold
apart what we imagine from what we perceive. An imaginary
and a perceived prowler, for example, are two vastly different

things for every householder. The extent to which we confuse what we imagine with what we perceive, as we sometimes do, is the measure of our inaccuracy and unreliability as observers— a grievous fault in scientific and legal matters.

To distinguish the two kinds or levels of imagination we shall call the one "primary" or "productive," and the other "second-ary" or "reproductive." The productive imagination is clearly prior to the reproductive: its work must precede that of the latter. Its raw materials are the impressions of sense as they are originally given in consciousness. The materials of the secondary imagination are sense qualities, i.e., these same sensations but as already processed by the primary imagination. Other differences will be noted hereafter.

But for all their differences they have a generic likeness which indicates that they have a common source in our one faculty of imagination. They are both activities or spontaneities of the mind; and they both deal with materials of sense. Active like thought, yet concrete like the senses, they lie intermediate, as it were, between thought and sensation, comprising a third faculty distinct from the latter two.

Although posterior to outer perception, the secondary imagination enjoys one distinct advantage; it is comparatively free whereas perception is bound. We cannot perceive what we will, but we can imagine just about what we please. This freedom disqualifies the imagination when we are concerned with accurate observation and reporting. But it is the quickening factor in another area of human life and interest, the realm of art. Here the spontaneity, originality, and power of the human imagination are most properly and impressively displayed in splendid edifices of sounds, words, colors, forms, stones. Here the imagination of man comes into its own and manifests an originative competence which is the wonder of all who reflect on it. May it not be that as the great world of art is the product of man's reproductive imagination, so the vast world of sense is the product of his productive imagination?

The hypothesis is alluring. It links the world of art in a most novel way with the world of experience, and draws them both from the same hidden spring of consciousness. It makes both art and world lively products of the mind and intimate reflections of its inwardness. Little wonder that Kant regarded the imagination as "an art hidden in the depths of the human soul." If he was not moved by these reflections when he penned his first *Critique,* he was probably moved by them when he penned his last.

Such, then, is the new theory of the human imagination with its two levels of operation. Setting aside the secondary level, let us turn to the primary level and follow the productive imagination through the several stages in the course of which it produces or "constitutes" perception.

3. Transformation and Projection

The first stage, as I remarked above, is that of transforming sense impressions into sense qualities. Now sense impressions in their original state are, like pains and aches, wholly private, inner, "subjective." Being thus immediate contents of consciousness they should fall, again like aches and pains, within the direct purview of introspection. Actually, however, we never grasp them by introspection. The instant we receive a sense impression we perceive a sense quality; a sound is always a sound *heard,* a color always a color *seen,* a tactual quality a quality *felt.* As mere sensations they would not thus belong to any department of the "external" senses but solely to the "internal" sense or introspection, along with aches and pains and all the other immanent contents of our private streams of consciousness. The first thing that perception or the primary imagination does, therefore, in transforming sensations into *outer* sense qualities is to remove them from the purview of introspection and to place them in one or other department of the external senses where alone they can be seen, heard, felt, etc.

This is a remarkable transformation, this change from inner impression to outer quality. It is remarkable because it involves a change from something nonspatial to something spatial. Whatever is internal to consciousness and within the realm of introspection is in every instance devoid of spatial extension. Aches and pains, sensations of pleasure and hunger, ideas, thoughts, feelings, all are grasped in my stream of consciousness as "inside" me, not "outside" me in space. If some of these are "localized" and thus associated with parts of my body, this is a feature added to them by me, not a feature they possess intrinsically. Intrinsically their only locus is my stream of consciousness and their only extension is that of duration in time. Of spatial extension and spatial locus they possess nothing inherently.

This difference between inner and outer, between nonspatial and spatial—or "unextended" and "extended," as Descartes put it—would seem to be so ultimate as to preclude any transforming of one into the other. Actually, we never observe any such transformation. Every time I reflect, I observe my inner data as inner, and outer data as outer; never do they even appear to change from one to the other. Nor do I see how they possibly could, any more than I can see how a color could change into a sound or vice versa.

In spite of this evidence, however, we are now to assume that certain, but only certain, of these inner data, namely, the "impressions of sense," undergo precisely this transformation, that somehow they are endowed with spatial extension—or "extensity" as some have called it as though to soften the blow—and are thus transformed in a flash into outer qualities standing before the external senses. *How* this takes place we cannot say;

it is "hidden in the depths of the human soul." It is sufficient for the theory of sensation to assume merely *that* it occurs, that it is a transformation involving 1) a change from nonspatial to spatial, or from nonextended to extended, and 2) a change of venue from inner to outer sense.

The second stage ensues forthwith. The transformed sense impressions, once invested with "extensity," are therewith "projected" outward and beheld as sense qualities "out there," filling space in all directions with an inexhaustible variety of hues and shades in endless combination, thus giving rise to the appearance of a sensible world with its host of sensible things.

Projection would seem to have been recognized by Descartes, although he did not label it "projection"; instead he compared it to the familiar psychological phenomenon of localizing pain. (Of transformation he seems to have been only dimly aware, as were most of his successors.)

The comparison will not hold up. For one thing, localization never extends beyond the limits of one's own body, normally at least, whereas projection extends to the uttermost limits of perceptual space. For another thing, a localized pain is never transformed from an inner sensation into an outer quality of things. A pain localized in a tooth, for example, is never projected as a quality of the tooth. The tooth can be observed and extracted; the pain cannot. No matter how precisely it may be localized a pain always retains its essential inwardness and privacy, whereas projected impressions lose completely their original inwardness and privacy and become instead outward and public qualities of things. By no effort can I thus transform sensations of pain; and by no effort can I refrain from projecting impressions of sense. The former remain ever within the domain of introspection; the latter appear in the departments of outer sense. Clearly, projection and localization are so different as to be quite beyond comparison.

The mechanics of projection are as concealed from us as are those of transformation. Here too we must content ourselves simply with assuming *that* projection takes place and that it supplements transformation. The two go manifestly together and constitute the first stage in the total process by which the primary imagination fashions out of sense impressions a world of sense experience. The end product of this first stage is outer sense qualities. At the next stage these are "combined," "assembled," "associated," "synthesized" into sense objects.

4. Synthesis of Object and Field

At this stage, too, we fail to catch the mind at work. From sense impression to sense object, through transformation, projection, and synthesis, the workings of the primary imagination are so concealed and sudden that we can only surmise from their end products what they must be like in transit.

These end products are sensible objects in a sensible world, the "real" things we experience, handle, live by and with. Now if these things are all groups of sense qualities, as the sensation theory holds, then the grouping in question must be of a singular nature. It cannot be the loose togetherness of juxtaposition, a casual association into which sense qualities may indifferently enter or not. It must be rather an intimate union, binding and compelling beyond our conscious control and impossible to dissolve once the fusion has taken place. Such a union may be called "real" or "objective," meaning thereby simply that the sense qualities thus fused have been transformed from an aggregate into a single thing (*res*) or "object."

If this object synthesis is a kind of fusion, it must be different from another kind of synthesis which gives us the field of objects. Now object and field go inseparably together. We never perceive a sense object in stark isolation, but always in a sensible

setting or horizon, in a field of environing sense objects. Correlatively, we never experience a field save as occupied by objects,
even though the only discernible objects be oneself and one's
space capsule. This is important to note because some have
spoken as though the field synthesis were subsequent to the object synthesis, as though we first combined sense qualities into
sense objects and then in similar fashion combined sense objects into a sensible world. If object and field go thus together,
the two corresponding syntheses must also go together; they
must be concurrent, not successive. More than this, they must
work intimately together. For, it will shortly appear that some
features of the field synthesis are involved in the fusion of objects, and that fusion in some form is ultimately involved in the
field synthesis.

As for the field itself, it has in every instance a luminous
center, the focus of perception, from which it shades off in all
directions becoming increasingly indistinct toward the periphery.
Center and periphery are permanent features of the field, but
their occupants are transient. With every shift of attention the
occupants change; what is at one time central may at another
time be peripheral, and conversely, depending on the direction
and focus of our gaze. This sensible field with its ever-shifting
foreground and background of sensible objects is none other
than the world of sense experience. Or, if in thought we isolate
it from its contents, it is the empirical space of the world.

Now if the field, too, is a product of synthesis, the synthesis
from which it arises is not that of fusion. We infer this from the
fact that the field is not itself a sense object but, precisely, the
"one field or horizon of sense objects," their all-embracing
"locus." Not being an individual sense object, the field is not
perceived in the same way that sense objects are perceived; its
very ubiquity precludes its being the focal point of any possible
perception. Still, as the ever-present setting of sense objects, as

the abiding center and periphery of every perceptual grasp, it is in some sense perceived every time we perceive any object whatsoever. We might say that in *perceiving* a sense object we are at the same time *coperceiving* the sensible world, the two in inseparable union. This indicates that the field synthesis is not only other than the object synthesis, fusion, but also simultaneous with it.

To say anything more specific about this field synthesis we must look more closely at the field itself. Now the field, although unmistakably one, is yet many-layered; it has a visual layer, an auditory layer, a tactual layer, as many layers as there are departments of sense. This suggests the possibility of peeling off one by one the various departmental layers, like an onion, until nothing is left. This is to say that if you were to remove the sensory stuff of which any layer is composed, then presumably you would remove also that layer. This would be the plight of persons born blind or deaf; to the extent that they are deprived of visual or auditory sensations their fields would presumably lack a visual or auditory layer.

From this layered structure of the field one would naturally assume a corresponding kind of synthesis by layering, a superposing of layer on layer in such a way as to bring about a kind of congruence such that qualities from different departments of sense could be made to occupy the same space, have the same locus, direction, reference. By this congruence the "same" surface can be both shiny and smooth, i.e., it can be a single surface possessing both visual and tactual qualities. Similarly, we can speak of seeing, hearing, touching, smelling, even tasting the "same" object. In these instances layering would appear to operate along with fusion in producing sense objects, and fusion with layering in making one the multilaminated field.

But more than this. Is not each departmental layer in turn the product of a prior synthesis? Must we not assume that the departmental layers cannot be superposed and brought to congruence until they have been separately formed? The manner of this formation would appear to be that of combining homogeneous sense qualities, colors with colors, sounds with sounds, tactual qualities with tactual qualities, so as to give rise individually to the various departmental layers. The qualities in this instance would seem to be juxtaposed, rather than superposed, inasmuch as like qualities are here projected side by side, so to speak, so as to spread out over the extension of the layer in question.

With these two phases of the field synthesis we would seem to be approaching the recognizable terrain of our common world of experience. The raw impressions of sense we have transformed and projected as sensible qualities and have synthesized these qualities by fusion, juxtaposition and superposition (or congruence) into a sensible field of sensible objects. But this field of objects still falls short of the empirical world. It has no past or future, no temporal extension. To give it a time dimension we must invoke a further stage of synthesis. Only then can our product emerge as the empirical world.

5. Synthesis and Time

Up to this point I have considered neither past nor future, only the present. All the materials acted on by the primary imagination have been taken as present, as present together at the same time, simultaneous or *tota simul*. From raw sensations through all the stages of the process up to sensory field and object there has been no passage of time beyond the duration of the original sensations themselves. Had there been a passage of time beyond this duration, the sensory ingredients at some stage in the process would have vanished, and no end product would have issued forth, no object or field.

So far, then, we have only a present object, a momentary object without past or future—I shall consider the field presently. But every present object has both past and future; it encompasses, even as present, previous moments each with its momentary fusion, and moments yet to come. This temporal fullness of the object entails a further and higher fusion of many successive momentary fusions spread out over a span of time which we call the duration of the object. Only thus can the object become a relatively permanent and enduring thing, as all objects are for us.

This higher fusion we may call the "synthesis of identity," inasmuch as by it the object acquires an identity which permits it to appear to us as the "same" object in many successive perceptions. Here memory and anticipation come into play, and with them arises the possibility of the familiar error of mistaken identity, an error which seems hardly possible in performing the mere momentary fusion. Thus at any given moment I may be correct in averring that I see this table; but I may be quite incorrect in believing that this table is the same table I saw here yesterday. Another one just like it may have been put in its place. On the other hand, if I am initially wrong about seeing a table at all, then my error is not one of mistaken identity; it is probably an illusion or hallucination.

Essentially the same considerations hold for the field. Each actual field must be as momentary as the sensations out of which it is wrought; it can endure only for the duration of its ingredients and with them must vanish into the past, to be followed by another equally momentary field, and this by yet another, and so on in the unremitting succession of time. Clearly, we must do with these momentary fields what we did with the momentary objects, much as we do with the successive frames of a movie film; combine them into the one vast field, or cinerama, of the sensible world. Only by this "cumulative" synthesis, as I shall call it, can the world acquire extension and continuity in time, as well as extension in space, and thus approximate the familiar world of our common experience.

In this cumulative synthesis, as in the synthesis of identity, memory and anticipation are involved. Here, too, a kind of mistaken identity is possible, as in the tragically distorted worlds of the paranoid or psychotic.

But the important point here is the role of memory and anticipation in the synthesis of identity and the cumulative synthesis. This role is indispensible because in both instances the materials to be synthesized are not simultaneous, but dispersed in time and hence not available for combination at any one moment. At any one moment only one field is present and actually available for processing; all the others are either past or future and thus apparently beyond the reach of the present operation. To be available at this present they must be remembered or anticipated. But to be remembered or anticipated is to be made only vicariously present, that is, to be "re-presented" by replicas or images supplied by memory and anticipation. Even if these replicas and images are accurate, they are still only residues or shadows of the actual fields which they represent. And, to the very extent that they are accurate, they are fixed with a lifeless permanence which may fit them for the record, so to speak, but which would totally unfit them for any present processing. Exactly the same for past and future objects. Like past and future fields, they too would seem not to be proper grist for the mill of the primary imagination.

How images of fields can literally be combined with an actually present field, or images of objects with an actually present object, is not at all clear. The previous stages offer no clue. For they all perform literal combinations of actual sense qualities with actual sense qualities, never actual sense qualities with mere images of sense qualities. They are fully actual in that their materials are actually present, not vicariously present in the form of images or representations supplied by memory or anticipation. The synthesis of identity and the cumulative synthesis, on the other hand, are not thus fully actual. There is about them an obscure quality of "inactuality," if I may so call it, or vicariousness, which sets them sharply apart from the preceding "momentary" syntheses.

6. The Primordial Time-Synthesis

But now these momentary syntheses become suspect. Kant suggests that all synthesis is time-synthesis, the gathering together of a manifold which has to be gone through in time and by this scanning process brought within the unity of a single apprehension. A familiar example of this would be looking at a statue from all sides as we walk around it, or "taking in" a large room simply by turning in one position. Here plainly a multitude of appearances or perspectives—momentary objects I have called them—is gone through in sequence and combined into the complex perception of statue or room. If what is here combined are the many perspectives given in succession, then their synthesis into a single object is clearly a time-synthesis, the synthesis of identity.

But what of each momentary perspective or object? Is it, too, precisely as momentary, the result of a time-synthesis, a time-synthesis prior to the synthesis of identity and the cumulative synthesis? Hitherto I have evaded this question. I have simply assumed a group of given momentary sensations and their momentary processing into a momentary object (or perspective) in a given momentary field. Of these momentary operations I remarked only that they take place simultaneously with the momentary sensations and persist only so long at these momentary sensations endure. This will no longer suffice. I must now ask how long these momentary sensations endure. What is the duration of the "momentary?"

If this duration is greater than zero, as it presumably is— that is, if it is not merely instantaneous, not merely "now"— then no matter how short it may be, it must have distinguishable instants dispersed over a time interval. The sensation, too, must be spread over this time interval; it must have a beginning and end and points in between. From first to last each point in turn becomes "now," all the other points being for that instant either before or after, gone or not yet, past or future. To scan this interval and to combine its successive materials into a "momentary" sensation, a primordial time-synthesis is plainly required, without which we would have no momentary sensations or impressions at all, but only an inchoate flux of sensory materials hopelessly jumbled together, occurring only for an instant, vanishing at once and giving way to another, and so on—a "manifold of sensibility" as Kant called it.

What this primordial time-synthesis is like we can infer, perhaps, from another time-synthesis which we can directly observe. Consider, for example, a tone as it is actually heard in its run-off from beginning to end—say, a single note in a familiar melody. Although the tone is strictly present only at each living "now" in its duration, still at each of these "nows" it is actually present as "just having been" and as "just about to be"—or "abouting to be" (we have no future participle in English). In other words, each "now" is more than a mere point-instant; it is rather a "living now," which shades off at both ends into an immediate before and an immediate after, a continuous shading off in which at one end the tone itself is retained, not recalled, and at the other "protained," not anticipated. I repeat, it is the tone itself that is retained and "protained," not an image of the tone: which means that the principal adjuncts here are not memory and anticipation with their supply of images, but their more primitive forms, which Husserl calls "retention" and "protention."* Once the tone has been thus perceived it may then be recalled or anticipated; and in the process of being recalled or anticipated it may— now as an image—repeat the original run-off with its succession of "nows" bound together by retention and protention.

Notice that we have been speaking here of a tone, not of an auditory sensation; speaking, too, of its perception, not its production as a sense object. This is important to bear in mind when, taking this observable process as a clue to what happens with unobservable sensations, we assume that in their run-off momentary sensations are the result of a similar time-synthesis, in this instance an unobservable, wholly conjectural, "primordial" time-synthesis. Here the process is no longer one of perceiving; for we do not perceive sensations; perception is still in the offing. Rather, the process is that of producing originally the momentary sensations out of which the primary imagination fashions perception and its object. The difference between the two syntheses is decisive.

The end product of the one synthesis is "having-heard-the-tone"; the end product of the other is a momentary sensation. Their raw materials are equally disparate. That of the synthesis in hearing is from beginning to end a tone heard. That of the assumed synthesis is not even a sensation, at least not a momentary sensation, since this is its end product. It must be something more primitive than sensations, a mere "manifold of sensibility." This manifold is at every instant an undifferentiated mass which vanishes as soon as it occurs, is succeeded in the "now" by another mass equally undifferentiated and instantaneous, and this by yet another mass, and so on in the unremitting flow of our conscious life. By hypothesis, this primitive

---

* See Husserl's *Ideas*, pars. 78 & 81; also his *Vorlesungen zur Phaenomenologie des inneren Zeitbewusstseins*, 1928.

flowing stuff is sensory; but it is not yet sensations. To get sensations out of it we must invoke a primordial time-synthesis. But before we can get this synthesis going we must first sift and differentiate out of the successive undifferentiated masses of sensory stuff just those homogeneous elements which will co-alesce into single momentary sensations—into auditory, visual, tactile sensations. This would seem to argue for some kind of instantaneous picking and choosing in accordance with fixed criteria of selection—an elaborate process prior even to the primordial time-synthesis and calling, I should think, for a sophisticated kind of equipment, which at this elementary level is all but unthinkable.

This, however, is not the only difficulty. Another arises when we ask as to the timing of those operations of the primary imagination which finally issue in perception and experience—transformation, projection, and the several syntheses. If the materials of these operations are momentary sensations, as we have assumed, and if momentary sensations are the end products of a primordial time-synthesis, then it would seem that the primary imagination can begin to operate only after these time-syntheses have completed their work. But once completed, a momentary sensation is over and done with; it is no longer avail-able for processing. Only an image of it supplied by memory would be thus available. This would render the whole operation of the primary imagination utterly inactual and vicarious, and, more important, rob it of any core of actuality, of being con-cretely present and "now." Plainly, this will not do.

If, on the other hand, sensations become available before the completion of the primordial time-synthesis—say, just after, or even as, it begins—then the above processes could start almost at once with the time-synthesis and run concurrently with it. In this event the sensory materials of these processes would not be momentary sensations, but the more primitive sensory stuff of the manifold. This would seem to render super-fluous the primordial time-synthesis and its resulting momentary sensations. All that is now required would be the primitive sensory stuff of the manifold and the instantaneous sifting of the homogeneous therefrom. This would entail, however, that the processes in question be also instantaneous, that from trans-formation and projection through the higher syntheses, from raw material to end product, no interval of time can elapse. There could be no lapse of time simply because the materials processed are ever merely "now," without duration, instan-taneous. Such an instantaneous processing eludes my under-standing completely.

And so, with or without the primordial time-synthesis, with or without momentary sensations, the operations of the primary imagination would seem to be incomprehensible, if not im-possible. The difficulty lies with their raw materials. These materials cannot be momentary sensations, for momentary sen-sations vanish at once on issuing from the primordial time-synthesis. And they cannot be instantaneous sensory manifolds, for this would entail that the operations, too, be instantaneous. Moreover, in both instances an instantaneous sifting of the ho-mogeneous would have to precede the whole process. Such are the difficulties that arise when we attempt to make clear the temporal character of the operations by which the primary imagination produces sense perception.

7. Two Kinds of Time-Synthesis

There was no such difficulty with the psychological time-synthesis in the hearing of a tone, principally because this syn-thesis is not productive, not a processing of raw materials into an end product. The synthesis here does not "produce" the tone. The tone itself is a sense object produced by the human voice or a musical instrument—according, at least, to the natural attitude. What is here synthesized is the "hearing-of-the-tone," our sense perception of the tone. Clearly, this synthesis is one with the act of hearing itself—an act, I repeat, which from beginning to end is an act of hearing, one act by virtue of the tone heard and a synthetic act by virtue of the retention and protention involved.

Similarly, with looking at the statue as we walk around it, and taking in the room as we turn on our heel, there is a succession in the seeing and a corresponding succession in what is seen, the successive perspectives. These visual perspectives lack the homogeneity of the simple tone. But for all their diversity they "add up" in precisely the same way, by retention and protention, into the seeing-of-the-statue or the seeing-of-the-room. Once again, what is here "synthesized" is not the objects seen or their perspectives. In no wise are these perspectives literally put together, combined as ingredients in an end product, the object. Like the phases of the tone they are "out there," products of an empirical situation in which they can be as readily photographed as seen by the human eye. Nor is it quite proper to speak of the act as "synthesized"; for it is itself a synthesis in the manner of retention and protention. What it synthesizes is not an alien raw material, but in a way itself as a single act of awareness. Putting it briefly, "synthesize" here is an intransitive, not a transitive verb.

This notion of an intransitive synthesis is much in need of further clarification. This need I shall attempt elsewhere to satisfy. For the present this much, I think, is clear. An intransitive synthesis is a kind of act or activity which Aristotle called *energeia* (plural, *energeiai*) and characterized as being complete and actual at every instance in its duration. It is complete in that its completion does not await the formation of an end product, and actual in that it is throughout an act of hearing, seeing, touching, smelling, tasting, or the like. A transitive or productive synthesis, by contrast, is not complete until the process is over and not fully actual until the end product is finished. All perception, inner as well as outer, is activity in this sense of *energeia*.

As an instance of a transitive or productive time-synthesis—a very important instance—consider our use of language. Take a simple utterance such as "It is raining." The utterance obviously takes time; it has a run-off beginning with the first syllable of the first word and ending with the last syllable of the last word. Since each syllable and word must be spoken in succession, a cumulative time-synthesis must be operating at each instant, retaining what has been traversed and "protaining" what is to come, and finally combining the dispersed elements into a single whole, the sentence as end product of the utterance. This productive synthesis, in Aristotle's terms, is not complete until the process is over and not actual until the surviving sentence is finished. In a way, the surviving sentence *is* the actuality of the utterance. It survives the utterance in that it can be endlessly repeated, translated, recorded, criticized, analyzed, and so on. It is to this extent a public object in the public domain of the intellect. Its objective status, to be sure, is not that of a physical or sense object; it is rather that of an ideal or intelligible thing. But it is nonetheless "real," as real as language itself, as science, knowledge, philosophy, and other such "objects" that go to make up the "cultural" dimension of human society.

If, on this very sketchy basis, I be allowed to say that for the natural attitude the empirically real contains things intelligible as well as sensible, things ideal as well as physical, I would then venture further to say that our mental activities with respect to these two kinds of objectives are correspondingly different; that with respect to things sensible or physical our perceptions are *energeiai,* nonproductive, and with respect of things ideal or intelligible, productive. Another way of saying this would be that we "discover" the sensible, but produce or "constitute" the intelligible. In the intelligible realm—this "noo-sphere," as Teilhard de Chardin called it in his *Phenomenon of Man*—we may say that the mind of man is a kind of *mens creatrix;* that in acquiring knowledge, for example, the knower must virtually produce or constitute his knowledge, though not for that reason the object known. In the sensible realm, on the other hand, the mind of man is not a maker or creator, but a discoverer, observer, explorer of what is already "there"—by acts which are all *energeiai,* but which can provide the basis for further productive acts of knowing.

With this schema, in spite of its oversimplification, we have a vantage point from which to view the whole program of this chapter, that of producing out of sensations the sensible world of experience. From this perspective the program would appear to be based on the erroneous assumption that all time-syntheses are productive, hence that the sensibility, like the intellect, must produce or constitute its objects in the acts of apprehending them. A curious feature of this assumption is that it applies only to outer or sense perception, not to inner perception. The reason for this, of course, is that only the former involves sensations. Thus it is another consequence of the sensation theory that it has obscured the distinction between productive and non-productive time-syntheses, acts that are constitutive and acts that are *energeiai.*

This completes my exposition of the productive process of constituting out of sensations a sensory world of experience. I began by following the intricacies of this assumed process through its hidden stages—transformation, projection, the syn-theses of fusion, juxtaposition, superposition, identity, and the final cumulative synthesis—right up to its end product, which alone is manifest, the sensory world of sensory objects. At this point I turned back on the material basis of the whole process, sensations, and observed that be they instantaneous or momentary, they involve insuperable difficulties, difficulties which spring from the failure to distinguish between time-syntheses which are productive and those which are not. In this wise is the initial "subjectivizing" of the sense qualities of things reversed by an assumed "objectivizing" performance of the primary imagination.

One final comment on this amazing performance. Viewed from the natural standpoint the performance would seem to have not one, but two end products: 1) our *experience* of the empirical world, and 2) the *empirical world* of our experience, the one being our own private acquisition, the other a vast public fact. But remember, we are moving within the framework of the theory of sensation and ideas and that, according to the theory of ideas, perception and object, experience and world, are not two, but one; that as "ideas" (*Vorstellungen,* etc.) they are the same. Hence we could confidently assume from the outset that in fashioning perception and experience out of sense impressions the mind was fashioning at the same time and out of the same materials the objects perceived and the world experienced. This in effect is what Kant proclaimed when he equated the conditions underlying the possibility of experience with those underlying the possibility of the objects of experience.

But if this equation of awareness and object is central to the theory of the productive process which I have just expounded, it is not central to another theory of the productive process which I have not expounded. I refer to Husserl's celebrated theory of "constitution," which differs sharply from Kant's theory on this very point: it restores the radical distinction between awareness and object which Kant's equation denies. With this important difference we have a clear basis for distinguishing an earlier and a later version of the productive process, a Kantian and a Husserlian version.

Having expounded the Kantian version I shall next turn to the Husserlian. Before doing so, however, I want to make a few remarks about the term "constitution" and about intentionality as the ground for Husserl's distinction between awareness and object.

8. Constitution: Kant

"Constitution" in the present context is plainly but another word for "formation," "construction," "production," "making," "fabricating," "fashioning," all of which are familiar terms signifying empirical processes of various kinds. To use these familiar terms is to invite empirical comparisons. But empirical comparisons are to be avoided because the hidden operations of the primary imagination are not empirical; they are pre-empirical or "transcendental," hence *sui generis*. It is desirable, therefore, to avoid these familiar terms with their empirical associations, and to employ the unfamiliar word "constitution" to signify the transcendental process of "constituting" sense experience out of sensations.

In the *Critique of Pure Reason* Kant did not use either the noun "constitution" or the verb "constitute." He used only the adjective *konstitutiv*. The mathematical principles of the pure understanding are *konstitutiv,* the dynamical principles only *regulativ,* with respect to phenomena (B, 296). With respect to empirical knowledge, however, he says later on (B, 692) that all the principles of the understanding are *konstitutiv,* whereas the principles of reason, the "ideas," are only *regulativ.* His covering definition here is that a principle is *konstitutiv* if it is a "principle of the possibility of the experience and the empirical knowledge of objects of sense" (B, 537). This is as far as Kant got with the word, although with the doctrine he attained to a classical formulation.

Fichte, Schelling, Hegel, and their successors in the German tradition were nearly as sparing as Kant in their use of the word "constitution." The doctrine, of course, they made thoroughly their own, each modifying it somewhat in his own way. Hegel's modification was perhaps the most important. He lifted the whole process of constitution out of the hidden depths of the individual subject, openly rebuilt its machinery with his logical "dialectic," deployed it as a cosmic "phenomenology of mind or spirit," and brought it to a grandiose consummation where history, metaphysics, and logic converge. In effecting this revolutionary shift from subjective consciousness to objective mind or spirit, Hegel also shifted his ground from perception to thought, from *Anschauung* to *Begriff*. With this shift "concept" replaced "sensation," and constitution took a turn which led it quite beyond the orbit of this essay on sensations. It is for this reason that I accord Hegel's majestic doctrine no more than this passing mention.

It was not until 1913 that the word "constitution" was brought to the prominence it now enjoys. In his *Ideen,* published in that year, Edmund Husserl used "constitution" to characterize one of the decisive features of his "Phenomenology." This characterization was doubly appropriate, for in expanding the use of a Kantian term Husserl was also effecting a radical revision of the Kantian doctrine.

9. *Constitution: Husserl*

This revision has to do initially with the traditional term "idea" and the ambiguity with which it is freighted. We noted several times how "idea" can stand for perception and perceived, experience and experienced, either or both. We noted, too, how by transfer the same ambiguity infects the words "perception" and "experience," how they too can stand indifferently for 1) the subjective process of perceiving or experiencing, and 2) the object perceived or experienced. It was this ambiguity, incidentally, which permitted Descartes in carrying out his methodical doubt to think away the existence of the sensible world and yet retain intact all his perceptions and experience of such a world. This is thinkable, of course, only if we assume that what we perceive or experience is indistinguishably one with perception and experience itself, i.e., if both are "ideas," *Vorstellungen, perceptiones* (as with Leibnitz).

To the natural attitude this ambiguity is unacceptable, because it denies in effect the distinction between our *awareness* of objects and the *objects* of which we are aware, a distinction which no one, I believe, will question when it comes to "outer" objects. All will agree that our private acts of awareness—perceiving, experiencing, imagining, remembering, thinking, feeling, and so on—are utterly distinct from the public objects to which these private acts refer. In these instances, at least, we distinguish unfailingly between awareness and object.

Husserl restored this distinction with his notion of "intentionality" and therewith dispelled at a stroke the disabling ambiguity in the traditional "idea." For intentionality makes imperative the radical distinction between *intending* act and *intended* object, as we shall see more clearly in the next chapter. Husserl never lost sight of this distinction. It was for him foundational. And this despite the fact that he persisted in using the German word *Vorstellung*. In translating *Vorstellung*, therefore, we must be careful with Husserl to render it not as "idea," but as "presentation" or "representation," indicating thereby that Husserl is not reverting to the traditional view with its inherent ambiguity.

Intentionality was lost to modern philosophy at its very inception; Descartes, perhaps under the influence of Suarez, abandoned it completely. Intentionality did not reappear until late in the nineteenth century with Brentano, Husserl's teacher. Husserl saw in it the "essence" of consciousness and made it the central tenet of his Phenomenology. In assuming this central role intentionality was destined to affect the whole doctrine of constitution beyond restoring the distinction between awareness and object. Let us glance briefly at the revision which it entailed.

In expounding the Kantian version of constitution I deliberately neglected what was uppermost in Kant's mind: namely, that the operations of the primary imagination are carried out under the aegis of reason, more specifically, under the blueprint of a set of categories, the supervision of a staff of schemata, and the high command of a transcendental unity of apperception. Important as this doubtless is, it was peripheral to my central concern with sensations and with the changes they must undergo when we assume that they are the raw materials out of which experience is wrought. Accordingly, in describing these changes I simply ascribed them to the operations of the primary imagination without any thought of a higher authority from which they might derive an intelligible rationale, a sovereign motive.

The question of such a higher authority, however, is bound to arise. Eventually we must ask why the mind should represent to itself an external world which is in fact internal to consciousness. Why should the mind confront itself with an independent existence which is not independent at all? Why should the mind fabricate a world and then take this world for "real"? On the face of it, it sounds like a vast self-deception. Is it?

Kant believed not and had an answer. His answer, in barest outline, is borrowed from Leibnitz's principle of *phaenomenon bene fundatum:* the phenomenal world constituted by mind is the genuine appearance of the noumenal world of things-in-themselves. Only thus is the phenomenal world truly appearance; without the noumenal world it would be not appearance but apparition, deception or illusion.

This is not Husserl's answer. Husserl's answer, also borrowed from Leibnitz, is based on Leibnitz's notion of "monad." This Husserl modified, rendered "radical," by infusing it with intentionality. According to Husserl, the monad is a closed system of inwardness which must preclude all outwardness For whatever is alleged to be external to the monad (or consciousness) must be "intended" as such and hence must really be internal. This is to say that to be intended is to be brought within the intending consciousness. Thus by virtue of its intentional essence consciousness is an "absolute" monad, absolute because "in principle" it excludes nothing—or includes everything.

Husserl's answer, then, is that it is the nature of consciousness to intend, to constitute, an "external" world; a consciousness not of this nature or essence is inconceivable. This points up, I think, the contrast between the answers which Kant and Husserl offer to the ultimate question of why the mind constitutes a world.

Clearly intentionality is the key to understanding Husserl's version of constitution. It is with intentionality, accordingly, that I shall begin my exposition of Husserl, bearing constantly in mind that constitution issued from the theory of sensation long before the advent, or reappearance, of intentionality.

VI
Intentionality and the
Intentional Relation

1. A Common-Sense View

Intentionality, according to Husserl, is the hallmark of consciousness. Consciousness alone possesses intentionality. By intentionality consciousness is unerringly to be distinguished from all other empirical phenomena.

To say that consciousness is intentional is to say that consciousness at the very least is "consciousness OF something." This, so to speak, is the minimum formula of consciousness. There is no such thing as mere "consciousness" or "awareness"; there is only consciousness OF something, awareness OF an object. Taking this as our basic formula, we would then have consciousness at its irreducible minimum as mere awareness or "cognition." Only infrequently are we thus merely aware. Usually we perform cognitive acts in conjunction with more complex acts of emotion and feeling and will. Cognition is here overlaid, as it were, with higher acts of evaluation and decision, which will not reduce to simple acts of awareness. To be angry at someone, for example, or to love someone, is to be more than merely aware of the person in question. Although more than cognitive, these higher acts all involve cognition as a basis or "founding level." We may say, then, that every act of consciousness either is or involves the awareness OF something as its object, i.e., it either is or involves an act of cognition.

Confining our attention to the elementary level of cognition we may then go on to note that to be aware of an object is in every instance to be doing something, to be active. Even when sunk in the deepest lassitude our faculties are yet at play; the most idle onlooking or daydreaming is still an activity we are carrying on. Since awareness is an act or activity of consciousness, it is most appropriately expressed by the use of an active verb. For this reason the verb "refer to" or "mean" is to be preferred to the lifeless expression "being OF." A still better locution is the classical word "intend," from which "intentional" and "intentionality" derive. To "be OF" or "refer to" or "mean" an object is to "intend" that object.

The Latin word *intentio,* from *intendere,* means etymologically a stretching out or reaching toward, implying an exertion of will. It is chiefly with this connotation of will that the English words "intend" and "intention" are used today, as when we say "I am not sure what he intends," or "His intentions are not clear." This connotation of will, however, must be reduced to a minimum when we use the word in its classic sense; we must allow it to connote nothing more than that we are directing our conscious glance at something as an object. This would concede that awareness, like all conscious activity, springs from an effort of will, that cognition is a voluntary act. But it would stress the fact that the volition here involved is solely cognitive in intent, that its aim is only to bring to awareness an object as such. Intention as cognitive act, therefore, is carefully to be distinguished from intention as deliberative act of will. Cognition is the more elementary act and underlies, as we have noted, all higher acts of will.

Intending, then, is an act or activity of consciousness and is best expressed as such by the active verb "intend." Now to intend an object is plainly to relate consciousness to that object, and that object to consciousness. This relation is the "intentional relation"—or OF-relation, awareness being OF its object—and is a structural feature of all intending. Although it is but a static feature of the active intending itself, this intentional relation is nonetheless essential to awareness; remove it and you remove awareness and all intending. But it is not similarly essential to the object of awareness; remove the relation and you remove the object "from consciousness," but you do not otherwise affect the object at all. If it be an empirical object, it is and remains what it was. Even if it be a purely imaginary object, it is still relatively independent of any given act of awareness, since we can bring it to awareness, i.e., imagine it repeatedly. These "unreal" objects I leave aside for the time being and confine my attention to the "real" objects of experience.

To these objects the intentional relation is quite unessential or "external," whereas to consciousness the intentional relation is, as already remarked, essential or "internal." Another way of saying this is that the intentional relation "really" relates awareness to its object, but only "nominally" relates the object to awareness. Being thus attached in very different ways to awareness and object the intentional relation is not reversible or symmetrical, but strictly irreversible or asymmetrical; it is strictly one-way and can properly be read in one direction only, as "awareness OF object," not as "object of awareness." When we reverse the order of the terms and read "object of awareness," we find that the relation expressed by "of" is not the same as that expressed by "OF" in the phrase "awareness OF object." For awareness is "OF" its object in the sense of intending it, whereas the object is "of" awareness not in the sense of intending anything, but in the passive sense of being intended *by* awareness.

This asymmetry of the intentional relation is plainly a consequence of the fact that it is awareness which does the intending, not the object. This is to say that the intentional relation takes its source in awareness and terminates in the object. Obviously it is anchored to its source as it is not to its terminus. It is, in a sense, the very core of awareness. It is not the core of the object. It merely touches the object from the outside, so to speak, remaining "external" so as not in any way to alter the object and thereby render it other than as it was intended, namely, as being just what it is.

Because of the asymmetry of the intentional relation, no act of awareness can be merely OF itself. A cognitive act that intended only itself would have solely its own intending to intend and hence would actually intend nothing at all. Clearly every act of awareness must be OF something other than itself. This inescapable otherness of act and object does not in the least preclude introspection or reflection. It simply says that in reflecting on acts of consciousness, the act reflected on must be numerically distinct from the reflecting act: that one act can be reflected on only by another act, and so on ad infinitum, as Spinoza correctly observed.

This otherness of act and object has a consequence of great importance. It implies that *actual* awareness requires originally the "givenness" of an independently existing object in order that consciousness may have anything to intend at all. For were there no such object originally "given," consciousness would have to remain an unactualized potency, for sheer lack of anything other than itself to intend. To remove this lack and to set consciousness off on its intentional career a real object must be given to consciousness *ab extra*. Only then, after this original awereness of the externally real, can consciousness turn on itself and discover the internally real. This would agree with Aristotle's dictum that there is no knowledge of the mind prior to the knowledge of things. This point is of signal importance, for it stresses two things: 1) the basic role of outer or sense perception, and 2) the primitive sense of perception generally as actually apprehending what is really "there" to be apprehended and "given" as such— "discovery," as I have called it.

The general purport of all this is unmistakable. It is that consciousness is not a windowless monad locked in the solitary confinement of its own sensations, ideas, and other inner contents. It is that consciousness, by virtue of its intentional essence, is a singularly transparent inwardness into which external existence can freely "shine," and which prior to this shining-in of the real is but an empty interior devoid of furniture. Consciousness on this intentional view is not closed to the real, but open to it, with as many openings as there are varieties of intending, beginning with sense perception and going on to memory, imagination, thought, conception, judgment, and so on. Intentional consciousness, in a word, is a non-monadic consciousness open to all that is; only a nonintentional consciousness can be closed, monadic.

Being open to all that is, consciousness can reach out and grasp, apprehend, comprehend, embrace—the metaphors are many—outer objects, the world and all that is. It does this, of course, only *intentionally,* not really or literally, that is, in the wholly unique manner of awareness. The world, on the other hand, embraces, comprehends consciousness really and literally, not intentionally. The contrast here between the adverbs "intentionally" and "really" reflects the corresponding contrast between the two ends of the intentional relation.

But what does it mean to be a content of consciousness intentionally? Does it mean that we have an "idea" of an outer object and that this "idea" somehow corresponds to the outer object, serving as its representative in consciousness? There is no place in this intentional view of consciousness for the "idea" in this traditional sense, or for the traditional "representative theory of perception." Outer objects are present to consciousness not by virtue of "ideas," but solely by virtue of the acts that intend them. The "idea," devoid of intention, therefore, must give way to the intentional act.

The difference between act and idea can hardly be exaggerated; it is as wide as the difference between the presence and absence of intentionality. An idea does not intend anything; an act intends its object. Or rather, an act *is* the intending of its object. In enacting the act, in performing or "living" the act, I am doing the intending; and what I intend is the object, not the act itself. In actually looking at a statue, for instance, I am looking at the statue, not at my looking. To be sure, I am not wholly oblivious of my act; but my awareness of it is quite peripheral, vague, more potential than actual and requiring a radical shift of attention to become fully actual. In the first instance, therefore, the act is not an object of awareness, but—precisely—an act of awareness. Only in the second instance, so to speak, does it become an actual object, when, namely, it is intended by a further act of reflection or introspection. It is thereupon discovered to be what it is, an act of intending, an inner "object" henceforth to be sharply distinguished from outer objects. Now if the basis of all intending is outer existence, as I argued above, we may then say that outer objects are objects of first intention and inner objects are objects of second intention. Not only acts but all that pertains essentially to them, intentionality, the intentional relation, and all, are objects of second intention.

The difference between act and idea becomes still more striking when we now note the dual nature of acts. Every act possesses an intrinsic quality in that it is at once both "real" and "intentional." This duality may be likened to a pair of dimensions; every act of awareness has a psychical ("real") and an intentional dimension, and both are vital.

Viewed in its psychical dimension an act of awareness is a real but passing event in a living stream of consciousness. In this stream, consisting mostly of acts, each act in due course is enacted and having been thus "lived" vanishes forthwith into an irretrievable past. As an act of consciousness it is, of course, an instance of an operation; i.e., it is a particular act of seeing or hearing, of perceiving or remembering, of imagining or thinking, and so on. To this extent each act shares in the permanence of the operation which it exemplifies. This permits us to identify its species and to give the act a date and a duration. But it discloses nothing more of the unique individuality of the act as a living segment of consciousness.

Only in the intentional dimension is this individuality fully displayed. An individual act of awareness is the actual intending of just this or that (real or imaginary, particular or general) object, and of nothing else. For example, I never merely see or imagine or think; I see this sheet of paper, imagine a unicorn, think of Julius Caesar. My act is never merely an instance of an operation; it is also a full, concrete intending of this or that object, exactly this and nothing else. It is, therefore, precisely this object—the paper, the unicorn, Julius Caesar—that makes my act in each instance what it actually and fully is. It is, I repeat, the object intended that gives my act the fullness of its individual being.

It is the office of the intentional relation to allow the object to exercise this vital role, to make the object willy nilly an integral part of the act itself. This is to say that since the intentionality of the act is its "being OF its object," its own being is to this extent one with the being of the object itself; the act *is* its object—intentionally. And since every act is a living segment of my conscious self, what I am doing in each act is "sharing" for the moment in the being of the object intended, becoming one with it—again, intentionally, not really. This, I think, is what Aristotle meant when he said that the soul in knowing becomes in a way the object known. The "way" in question is the utterly unique way of intentionality.

Only when viewed under both dimensions does the act of awareness reveal the qualities of the living process which it actually is. Sharing *really* in the being of the self or psyche and *intentionally* in the being of the object, its own being is that of an entity which cannot be itself without being also an other (the object which it is "OF"). This peculiar duality of being both self and other* is particularly striking with objects of first intention. To say, in these instances, that "being an other" is only intentional, not real, is not to say that it is fictional or imaginary or unreal *to the act*. It is rather to emphasize the uniqueness of the intentional act as a being which preserves the distinctness of self and other while yet allowing the other, even in its distinctness, to enter into the composition of the self. To grasp this is to grasp intentionality, the intentional relation, the act of awareness, being as "being OF" its object. It is also to understand how and why intentional consciousness is not a monad sealed within itself, but an avid openness to all that is, a limitless capacity of "becoming" all things.

This brings to a head my sketch of intentionality. My aim being not completeness, but synopsis, I concentrated in a quite general way on intentionality as the essential and distinguishing feature of consciousness, consciousness as a minimum, mere cognition or awareness. This deployed itself in a number of

---

*Is this perchance what Plato had in mind when in the *Timaeus* he constituted the world soul and the souls of men out of the "circle of the same" and the "circle of the other"?

themes: intending as the primordial activity of consciousness; the intentional act as the unit of this activity (and its difference from "idea"); the intentional relation with its asymmetry; the nature of intentional being (becoming intentionally the object, the object becoming intentionally a "content"); and lastly, our intentional involvement from the beginning with otherness and existence. In treating of these themes I looked chiefly at the species of intentionality called outer or sense perception with its objects of first intention. Of the many other genera and species I made only the barest mention, not even noting the important difference between perceptual intending on the one hand and conceptual and judgmental intending on the other. But for all these deficiencies I think I have made clear in outline the sharp contrast between an intentional view of consciousness and the traditional view of mind as a receptacle of sensations and ideas.

One further word. Intentionality as I conceive it is an empirical phenomenon, a feature of the natural world to be observed and described in the natural attitude. But it is a most singular feature. It springs only from psychic centers whence it radiates outward bathing the world in a glow of apprehension, so to speak, making it for the first time an "object" in the sense of an "object of consciousness." The transformation, to be sure, is hardly more than nominal; nothing is really changed save the psychic centers. And yet, all is vastly different, as different as light from darkness. For in evolving these psychic centers, the world has rendered itself luminous to consciousness, transparent to natural inquiry. In doing this the world has added to its original "being" the further sense of "being known." Or, it has added to its "real" dimension an "intentional" dimension and therewith cloaked itself in a veritable "noosphere," to use once again the suggestive term of Teilhard de Chardin. But enough! My point is that intentionality is not only a psychic phenomenon; it is also a cosmic phenomenon. In its cosmic aspect it is that dimension of the real which provides the meeting place of self and world, subject and object, mind and matter, inner and outer, and other monadic opposites. As the great conciliating medium intentionality is one of the neglected wonders of creation, perhaps the profoundest of all commonplaces, and surely one of the central themes for any theory of mind and man.

The contrast between this intentional view of consciousness with its two dimensions and the traditional monadic view with its single dimension is now evident. The traditional view was introduced by Descartes when he took to sensations and ideas. If he learned anything about *intentio* from his scholastic training at La Fleche, he rejected it out of hand. For in relating sensations to outer things as effects to causes, he denied by implication that they are intentionally related as awareness to object. In effect, then, Descartes replaced the intentional relation with the causal relation and thereby denied to ideas their cognitive character, their intentional function. Thus deprived, ideas shrank to the status of contents in the stream of consciousness, contents wherein awareness and object are somehow one. With intentionality this ambiguous oneness of awareness and object would have been impossible; without intentionality it was almost inevitable. And so it was the neglect of intentionality, as much as anything else, which gave license to the new theory of sensations and ideas.

2. Husserl's View

Husserl would not agree with this account of intentionality. He would agree that consciousness is indeed intentional, that intentionality involves an intentional relation between act and object, and that this intentional relation involves in turn the sharp distinction between awareness and object. But he would flatly oppose what I said about the intentional relation: 1) that it is real at the subject end, but nominal at the object end; and 2) that in outer perception consciousness contains its object only intentionally, not really. He would stoutly maintain the opposite: 1) that the intentional relation is real at both ends; and consequently 2) that in outer perception consciousness contains its object really, not merely intentionally.*

I use here the conditional "would" because Husserl did not expressly reject the two theses which I espoused and did not explicitly formulate his own theses in opposition. He was apparently quite unaware of "my" theses and hence of any opposition to his own. Being unaware of this opposition he was not moved to state his own theses. Had he done so, he would have examined carefully the logical properties of the intentional relation and particularly how it attaches to its object. This he did not do. Instead, he simply took it quietly for granted that the intentional relation is internal to both act and object— though doubtless not in exactly the same way—and inferred from this that the object, no less than the act, must be "internal" to consciousness. This inference he stated explicitly. In making this explicit statement he was averring implicitly that consciousness contains its object not merely intentionally but really, and this because the intentional relation is real at both ends. It is only by implication, then, that Husserl holds to the two theses

*I find it difficult to avoid this dual use of "real" in opposing it to both "nominal" and "intentional." If "real" means the same in both instances, "nominal" and "intentional" too would presumably mean the same or very nearly the same. In fact, "nominal" and "intentional" do mean much the same. And yet, there is a difference, if only a nuance, which is desirable to stress in referring 1) to the way in which the intentional relation attaches to its object, and 2) to the way in which consciousness includes its object. It is preferable, I think, to say that the intentional relation attaches only "nominally" or "externally" (rather than "intentionally") to its object, and that consciousness includes its outer object only "intentionally" (rather than "nominally").

which I ascribe to him, and by implication that he opposes mine. Let us take a closer look at Husserl's theses and their consequences.

Husserl's theses are connected as ground and consequence. If the intentional relation is real or internal to the object, as it is to the act (the first thesis), then this relation must bind act and object together in a real unity which can be no other than a unity of consciousness, since intending springs from consciousness alone, hence consciousness must really contain its object (second thesis). The first thesis leads to the second; the second follows from the first. From the two thus conjoined follows a third, the grand thesis of transcendental phenomenology, that all intending of outer objects is constituting. For if consciousness really contains its object, then obviously the object must be a product or "accomplishment" (*Leistung*) of consciousness, a mere "intentional correlate" constituted by the intending act. The perceived object, in other words, must be a "presentation" or *Vorstellung*—though not an "idea" in the traditional sense.

Notice now what follows. Act and object are really contained in consciousness. They differ, nonetheless, as intending from intended. Clearly, they must occupy correspondingly different strata or dimensions of consciousness. The one dimension is that of the so-called "stream of consciousness," the only dimension recognized by the tradition. The other dimension, first recognized by Husserl, is that of the object as constituted *Vorstellung*. Husserl was tireless in insisting that the object perceived is not a "content" of our stream of consciousness. Only the act is "immanent" in the stream; the object is "transcendent" of the stream. Mark well that the object is transcendent only of the stream; it is not transcendent of consciousness itself. Consciousness itself, accordingly, has the two dimensions of "immanence" and "transcendence," or "noesis" and "noema," as Husserl later called them. Immanent noesis and transcendent noema correspond as intending act and intended correlate.

With this distinction between immanence and transcendence Husserl has enlarged by a whole dimension the traditional view of consciousness and brought to systematic clarity the distinction between awareness and object. In doing this he has also equipped consciousness for the role of all-container, of absolute monad. For if all that is intended must be internal to consciousness, precisely because it is intended—and what, indeed, cannot be intended by consciousness in some fashion or other?—then plainly consciousness must really contain all that is, either as immanent act or transcendent thing. This implies that there is nothing, literally nothing, "outside," or "external" to, consciousness. This is the realm of sheer nonbeing; consciousness is the realm of being. And so Husserl's doctrine of constitution is also a doctrine of radical monadism.

Husserl's dimensions of immanence and transcendence do not correspond to the two dimensions which my theses involve. The act, I said, has a real or psychic dimension in being a real event in the stream of consciousness. It has also an intentional dimension in being that through which consciousness becomes one with its object (intentionally, not really), whence consciousness may be said to contain its object only intentionally, not really. The one dimension is strictly real, the other just as strictly intentional. Husserl does not recognize a strictly intentional dimension. His immanent dimension may be as real as my psychic dimension. But his transcendent dimension is not in the same sense intentional at all; it is on the contrary real, real in the sense that consciousness really (not merely intentionally) contains its object. Neither of Husserl's dimensions is intentional as opposed to real; they are both real. For Husserl, accordingly, intentionality is not a dimension; it is rather the relation between the two dimensions of consciousness, between immanent noesis and transcendent noema, constituting process and constituted product.

This leads to a further difference between Husserl's view and mine. On my view both act and consciousness are two-dimensional; the act as act-of-consciousness is so far one with consciousness as to share the essential features of consciousness, namely, its real and intentional dimensions. On Husserl's view only consciousness is two-dimensional; the act has but one dimension, that of immanence. As immanent event the act is sharply distinguished from its corresponding transcendent noema, as sharply as awareness from its object. Plainly, consciousness alone possesses the two dimensions of immanence and transcendence; the act possesses but one, immanence.

Husserl's act with its one immanent dimension is manifestly a very different thing from the act I described above with its real and intentional dimensions. Husserl's act, having no intentional dimension, is intentional only in the sense of constituting its object or noema. This means simply that Husserl has equated intending and constituting; to intend an (outer) object is to constitute that object, and conversely. Furthermore, this constituting is a "real" process of "really" making a "real" noema which is "really" contained in consciousness. "Real" has here, of course, the two senses of immanence and transcendence. But in both senses it is opposed to intentional as I have construed it. There is no room for my sense of intentional. All is real. Intentionality for Husserl is not the (intentional) sharing of all being or existence; it is not the meeting place of self and other, subject and object; it is not a cosmic as well as a psychic dimension. It is exclusively a feature of a closed transcendental consciousness, its essential feature, that feature by virtue of which transcendental consciousness creates for itself a world and all that is and thus displays itself as an absolute, all-compassing monad.

Husserl's equating of intending and constituting does not seem to hold for inner perception; objects of second intention do not seem to be constituted by introspection or reflection.

This is but to say, of course, that the constituting process is not itself constituted. In this event, inner intending would not be constituting, but discovering, perceiving. Assuming there would be no disagreement on this point, I shall leave it and return to the intending of outer objects, where the equation holds.

This equation, which is in a way the core of Husserl's theory of constitution, follows, as I remarked above, from his first two theses. Since 1) the intentional relation is internal to the object as well as to the act, hence 2) every intended object must be really internal to consciousness and thus 3) must also be a product of consciousness; therefore: intending $=$ constituting. If this be the order of priority, it would also be the order which Husserl might be expected to follow in arguing for his theory of transcendental constitution.

But, once again, Husserl never stated and never argued for the primary thesis that the intentional relation is real at both ends. He did, however, argue explicitly for the second thesis that outer objects must be internal to consciousness. In doing this he was assuming implicitly the first thesis as a suppressed premise. It is this that I want to expose in the next chapter, where I shall examine Husserl's arguments for the second thesis.

These arguments are of two kinds. The one kind, the more detailed and specific, is that of the "transcendental reduction," the central aim of which is to show that the alleged "outer" object of sense perception must be, as intended, an "intentional accomplishment" (*Leistung*) of the intending consciousness. The second kind, the less detailed and more general, was set forth on at least three separate occasions. In each of them Husserl attempts to show that a so-called "outer" object on becoming an "object of consciousness" must become thereby "internal" to consciousness.

It will be convenient to distinguish the argument of the reduction as "special" from the latter argument as "general." In the history of natural science the special argument or theory usually precedes the general. The special theory of relativity, for example, preceded by some years the general theory. My feeling is that with Husserl the general preceded the special, for reasons which I shall later disclose. But this is of little moment here. Since I must adopt some order, I shall examine first the general argument and then the special argument.

It may be well to remark that in both arguments Husserl begins with the natural attitude. He was not one to berate the natural attitude and its naive realism. It is one of the merits of Husserl's phenomenology that it springs from the natural attitude and from a deep respect for its deliverances. Where else, indeed, do we initially encounter "phenomena," the "things themselves"? Eventually, to be sure, Husserl abandons the natural standpoint, but only for reasons which the natural standpoint itself allegedly provides. Our attention, therefore, will focus intently on these alleged reasons, these natural deliverances or insights, which impelled Husserl to abandon the natural standpoint and to repair to the transcendental standpoint. Are these reasons genuine insights; or are they inferences from unstated premises, such as the premise that the intentional relation is real at both ends?

VII
Is the World Internal to Consciousness?

1. The General Argument

The three occasions on which Husserl sets forth his general argument for the internality of outer objects are 1) his own special preface to the English edition of the *Ideas,* 2) the article "Phenomenology," which he wrote for the *Encyclopædia Britannica,* and 3) the first of the five *Cartesian Meditations.* Since the three versions do not differ in any material respect, there is no need to examine each in detail. The *Britannica* article is the most forceful statement of the argument. It is this version, therefore, that I shall chiefly consider. Unless otherwise stated all quotations in this section will be from the *Britannica* article.

The argument begins, in each instance, with the natural attitude of common sense. In this attitude the world exists for us as a reality independent of our experience of it and inclusive of us all. This natural attitude is quite satisfactory for the ordinary purposes of "life and science"; but it is unsatisfactory for philosophical reflection. It is unsatisfactory because philosophical reflection finds itself "impelled beyond the positive realism of life and science" by an "insight," provided by the natural standpoint itself, that the world, naively taken for independently real, cannot really be independent of consciousness at all. For the moment we let this "independent" world "make its 'appearance' in consciousness as 'the' world, it is thenceforth *related to the subjective;* and all its existence, and the manner of it, assumes a new dimension" (my italics). It is on this "new dimension" that philosophical reflection now focuses. What it discovers is that on being made the object of consciousness the world becomes "related to consciousness" and acquires thereby a " 'being for us' . . . which can only gain its significance 'subjectively' "

By virtue of being "related to consciousness" the being of the experienced world reveals itself as "being for us," a "being for consciousness," a relative, not an independent, being. Into this relative being the naive independence of the empirical world dissolves under the analytic scrutiny of phenomenological reflection; this independence is now seen to be a merely putative independence, a quality imputed to the world, i.e., the world is "posited" by the consciousness which makes the world its object. "Making," therewith, ceases to be a metaphor and acquires a literal meaning: consciousness in originally intending the world literally makes or "constitutes" the world as its own intentional product and contains it as an integral part of itself. To this extent the world is "internal" to consciousness, and "we may call the world 'internal' *because it is related to consciousness"* (my italics), and because, too, this *"relativity to consciousness* is not only an actual quality of our world, but from eidetic necessity, the quality of every conceivable world" (my italics), i.e., every conceivable world must be a possible object of consciousness, must be necessarily related to consciousness.

The whole burden of this argument lies plainly in the repeated statement that the world is "related to consciousness," in the sense of being an object of consciousness, a fact which can hardly be debated. But it can be debated whether this relation is what Husserl obviously takes it to be, namely, real to both world and consciousness. This is by no means so evident as to be beyond question. It is surprising that an inquirer so acute as Husserl should overlook this point entirely, should not once consider even the possibility that the intentional relation may be external to its object and that consciousness may thus contain its object only intentionally, not really. As though unaware of this possibility Husserl simply takes it for granted that the intentional relation is real to its object and concludes without further ado that consciousness must really contain the world. The rest then follows, as we now well know.

Such is the "insight" which, according to the general argument, impels beyond the natural attitude to the transcendental standpoint. From the natural standpoint, of course, it is not an insight, but an oversight, a mistake of momentous consequence. The cause of the mistake, I strongly suspect, is Husserl's unquestioning adherence to the theory of sensation and the monadic view of consciousness—perhaps, too, his uncritical acceptance of the Hegelian doctrine, then widely held, that all relations are internal.

2. The Special Arguments

The general argument dealt not so much with a single species of awareness as with the intentionality of outer experience in general. The special argument, as its name would indicate, deals with a single species of intentional consciousness, namely, sense perception. Since it is more specific, it is naturally more detailed and technical. This argument evolved in Husserl's mind in the course of the *Logical Investigations* and emerged fully developed in the *Ideas,* where as the celebrated transcendental "reduction," it received its most authoritative and incisive formulation. In examining the argument I shall quote from the *Ideas,* unless otherwise indicated, as translated into English by Boyce Gibson, albeit with frequent emendations of my own wherever a more accurate and literal rendering seems to require it. I shall use the pagination of the 1931 edition, published by George Allen & Unwin Ltd. Since Husserl was rather lavish in his use of italics, I shall indicate explicitly only those italics which are mine; where no such explicit indication is given the reader is to assume that the italics are Husserl's.

The special argument—that consciousness must really contain its objects—is twofold; it has two parts relatively independent of each other, yet intimately connected. The first part is set forth in the First Chapter of the Second Section of the *Ideas* (pp. 101-111, paragraphs 27 through 32). The second part is set forth in the succeeding chapter, the Second Chapter of the Second Section (pp. 112-146, paragraphs 33 through 46). Both parts set out from the natural attitude but deal with different features thereof. The first part dwells on the "general thesis" which the natural standpoint is said to involve. The second part focuses on the way in which outer objects are "given" to consciousness. Briefly, the first part argues from "thesis" or "positing," the second from "givenness"; and both conclude that what we regard as "outer" must really be "internal" to consciousness. I shall examine first the argument from thesis and then the argument from givenness.

A. THE ARGUMENT FROM THESIS

Up to this point I have made no mention of "thesis" or "positing" or of their connection with "constitution." The connection with constitution is close. According to the theory of constitution outer objects are fashioned out of sensations. But even when thus fully fashioned or constituted they still lack one vital competent, namely, "existence." Now existence, as Kant insisted, is not a "real predicate," i.e., not an actual constituent of a thing, hence not a product of synthesis or constitution, but a result of "positing" or "thesis." Thesis is thus something over and beyond the constituting act itself, something that must supervene on the act in order that the product of the act may be rendered an "existing" thing, an "independent" object "out there" in the external world. Until it has this "sense" of existing independently out there, the merely constituted object is not the object we encounter in the natural attitude. The doctrine of constitution, therefore, requires to be supplemented by the doctrine of thesis—a requirement which Husserl was the first to emphasize.

But if constitution requires thesis, thesis also requires constitution, since, presumably, it is only something constituted that can be posited. This mutual connection is important; for if we can show that sense perception involves thesis, we can infer at once that it also involves constitution. And, conversely, if it involves constitution, it must also involve thesis. In either event, —and a fortiori in both—the conclusion is inescapable that consciousness must really contain its objects.

Let us take a closer look at "thesis" and "positing" and their equivalence. These two words are derived from equivalent Greek and Latin verbs, both of which mean to put, place, or set. "Thesis" is transliterated from the Greek θέσις, (from τίθημι); "positing" is taken almost as directly from the Latin positio (from pono). Since τίθημι and pono have the same meaning, it is etymologically correct to equate thesis and positing.

To English ears, however, this equation has an unfamiliar ring. Thesis, as we customarily use it, does not directly suggest positing; and positing, infrequently used at best, does not directly suggest thesis. Positing came to us from the medieval schoolmen, chiefly, I believe, from their logical writings. In the modus ponens, or modus ponendo ponens, for example, one spoke—in the corresponding Latin, of course—of "positing" the antecedent of a hypothetical proposition and hence of being forced to "posit" the consequent, whence the *ponens* in the title. In contemporary English we would say "affirm" or "assert" rather than "posit"; and we would not speak of the "thesis" of antecedent or consequent. Positing and thesis have come to mean something so different for us that we can recover their sameness only by an effort.

In German usage, on the other hand, this sameness or equivalence has been preserved. Both *Thesis* and *Position*—all German nouns are capitalized—retain the active sense of placing, putting, setting as a purely mental act, an act of thought or understanding, like the positing of the antecedent. Note that the German *Position* is the equivalent of the English "positing," not of the English "position" and is to be translated accordingly. To *Thesis* and *Position,* both of foreign extraction, German philosophers added three other equivalents of strictly German origin: *Setzen, Setzung,* and not infrequently *Satz*. These five terms are virtual synonyms. They all express the one central notion of putting or placing *as an activity of consciousness;* more especially, in German philosophical usage, the activity or act of positing existence.

This philosophical usage goes back at least to Kant, to his famous dictum that "existence is not a real predicate," but "only the positing of a thing" (*bloss die Position eines Dinges, K.d.r.V.,* B 626, A 598. Cf. also B 287 n.). What Kant here means by *Position,* "positing," is clear enough. It is plainly equated in the context with *Setzung,* which signifies that empirical existence is something "posited" by consciousness, the result of a "thesis." Fichte makes capital of this notion in his *Grundlage der gesamten Wissenschaftslehre* (cf. especially *Erster Teil,* 3). He makes positing (*Setzung, Setzen*) the principal "activity of the ego" (*Handlung des Ich*). In characterizing this *Handlung,* however, Fichte prefers *Thesis* to *Position,* for he finds that the *Setzen* which the ego performs advances in three phases: "thesis," "antithesis," and "synthesis." He may have got this triad from Kant's *obiter dictum* about the way the three categories are related in each of the four groups. It became, in any event, the famous triad of Hegel's dialectic, surely one of the most distinctive products of German philosophical thought.

Little wonder that "thesis" and "positing" (*Position*) are a bit disconcerting to English readers. Not only are they unfamiliar; their credentials are suspect; and the metaphysical load they bear is highly preemptive: all empirical existence, they declare, is "only a positing" performed by consciousness!

Manifestly we are dealing here with another one of those "fundamental assumptions," another philosophic predilection like the theory of sensation. Unlike the sensation theory, however, this "thesis" predilection is restricted in the main to the German idealistic tradition. Its genealogy, nonetheless, goes back to the theory of sensation and ideas from which, as we have observed, constitution, thesis, and finally monadism ensue. Husserl's Transcendental Phenomenology is perhaps the most complete and striking phase of this development. In it we witness, as Father Lauer put it, the final "triumph of subjectivity," the consummation of the subjectivizing process which began with Descartes.

And so in the very terms he takes as primitive—"thesis" and "positing"—Husserl has quietly and unobtrusively affirmed at the outset what his argument ostensibly would prove as a consequent. For if empirical existence is extruded by positing, then assuredly what we naively call "outer" must in sooth be internal to consciousness, i.e., consciousness must really contain its objects. I have no doubt that to Husserl this positing seemed to be pretheoretically evident, self-evident. But is it not the same dubious self-evidence that attaches to sensations, the self-evidence of a predilection, Let us now turn to Husserl's argument from thesis.

The argument from thesis begins in the natural attitude with "a piece of pure description *prior to all* 'theory' " (p. 105); namely, the essence of the natural standpoint is "the general thesis (*die Generalthesis*) by virtue of which the world is ever-present to me as the all-encompassing reality embracing all existence" (p. 107). The evidence for this statement is immediate and direct; we need only turn our reflective gaze on the "essence" of the natural attitude. Thus prior to all theory, prior to all inference, hypothesis, argument, it is pretheoretically evident, self-evident to the natural standpoint itself, that the living core of this standpoint is a "general thesis."

In itself this general thesis "does *not* consist *in an act proper* (*ein eigener Act*), in an articulated judgment about existence" (p. 107). It is rather "something persistently enduring (*etwas . . . dauernd Bestehendes*)" throughout the course of our waking lives, giving to all that we perceive "the character of being 'there,' 'present,' and capable at all times of rising to the level of articulate speech." Thus even though it is not an "act proper," still "we can treat this potential and unexpressed thesis exactly as we can the thesis of an explicit judgment" (ibid.), namely, we can "suspend" it.

The argument now turns on an alleged similarity between judgment and perception, intellect and sense. Both are said to involve thesis, a thesis which in both instances can be "suspended." Presumably, the instance of judgment is the more evident, or familiar, and hence is to be taken as the touchstone for the less evident instance of perception. It may be well here to recall another "similarity" between judgment and perception which we previously examined and found wanting. Let us keep this previous instance in mind as we examine the present "similarity."

Judgmental thesis is most easily discerned in the phenomenon of "suspending judgment." When we suspend a judgment we lay aside for the time being our acceptance or rejection of it, and simply "entertain" it as a mere statement or proposition, usually for the purpose of clarifying or explicating its meaning, setting forth its antecedents and consequences, etc., all with an air of complete detachment. Having examined the proposition in this withdrawn manner we may then lift the suspension and once again declare our assent or dissent. Or, as sometimes happens, we may be left in doubt by the examination and be moved to defer our commitment pending the receipt of further evidence. In this event we do not lift the suspension, but continue it, this time, however, with the hope of lifting it eventually and thus removing a state of indecision.

This element of belief or commitment, actually holding to be true or false, probable or impossible, etc., is the element of thesis in judging which Husserl has in mind. It is plainly not an act proper, like the act of framing (or constituting) a proposition. And yet it is just as plainly a performance of some sort, a performance vital to judgment and, indeed, to the conduct of life. We might say that it makes the judgment a judgment, so that without the thesis, or with the thesis suspended, the judgment is no longer a judgment, but a proposition. It will be convenient here to distinguish the two on this basis: a judgment is a proposition plus thesis; a proposition is a judgment minus thesis.

Obviously the thesis adds nothing material to the proposition; and its suspension subtracts nothing material from the judgment. Materially, judgment and proposition are not merely the same, they are literally identical. What suspending the thesis does to judgment, therefore, is simply to render it inoperative in a state of suspended animation, so to speak, set it in "brackets," as Husserl puts it, or "out of gear" *(ausgeschaltet)*.

Now it is Husserl's contention that as we can suspend any judgment thesis, so in "exactly" the same way can we suspend the general thesis of the natural attitude, the thesis that "posits existence," the empirical existence of the world. *"We put out of action the general thesis which belongs to the essence of the natural attitude,* we place in brackets all that it includes in re-spect of existence *(in ontischer Hinsicht)*, i.e., the *whole natural world* which is continually 'there for us,' 'present,' and will ever remain there as 'reality' for consciousness even though we choose to bracket it" (p. 110).

"If I do this, as I am fully free to do, I do *not* then *deny* this 'world' as though I were a sophist; *I do not doubt its exis-tence* as though I were a sceptic; rather I exercise 'phenomeno-logical' ἐποχή which completely bars me from using any judg-ment *(Urteil)* [sic] concerning *spatio-temporal existence"* (p. 110).

I added a "sic" toward the close of this quotation to call at-tention to the word "judgment." The phenomenological suspen-sion of the general thesis "completely bars me from using any *judgment* concerning spatio-temporal existence" (my italics). All *judgments* which assert or deny or imply such existence are debarred. Does the phenomenological suspension do anything more than outlaw these existential *judgments?* Is it anything more than a *judgmental* suspension?

This question is decisive, for if there is no such thing as the general thesis, if it is a groundless assumption, then Husserl's reduction can only be judgmental. It could affect only the judg-ment, "the world exists," not the actual existence of the world. In this event, Husserl's reduction would be much the same as Descartes's "methodical doubt" of the world's existence. It is in effect, however, Husserl's contention that this is precisely where he goes beyond Descartes, that whereas Descartes was content with suspending merely the judgment, "the world exists," he (Husserl) was intent on suspending also the actual existence of the world, thus adding to Descartes's judgmental suspension a sweeping experiential or perceptual suspension.

Manifestly, this "radical" addition is possible only on the assumption of the "general thesis," an assumption which never occurred to Descartes. It was not until Kant that the notion of thesis came to the fore. In this respect Husserl's attitude toward Descartes was a bit anachronistic. It was not, however, uncharitable; for Husserl felt that the genius of Descartes was so "original" that he might well have discerned a feature so "self-evident" and decisive. All of which is to say, of course, that for Husserl the general thesis is obvious beyond question and that the reduction is a literal suspending of existence, as well as a suspending of existential judgments, that is, an experiential as well as a judgmental suspension.

Being literally a suspending of the "general thesis," the phenomenological reduction should affect the objects of the natural attitude much as the judgmental suspension affects judgments. As the suspended judgment is no longer a judgment but a proposition, so the suspended natural object should be no longer a natural object but something different—different not in its content, for by analogy this should remain exactly the same, but different in its existence, namely, with its existence suspended or "neutralized." The difference might be put this way: the reduced "natural object" is no longer "natural" but simply an "object"—yet still an "object of perception" or "perceptual object."

We have, then, the "perceived natural object" and the mere "perceptual object" to which the former reduces. Since both objects involve perception, one might naturally suppose that both are perceived. But not so. What we actually perceive is solely the "perceived natural object." We do not perceive the "perceptual object"; we grasp it only by "transcendental reflection," a kind of reflection which comes into play only after suspending the general thesis, not before, i.e., not in the natural attitude. What we thus grasp is no longer natural, existent, real, but just that which is posited as natural, existent, real. This is to say that the perceptual object is the "content" of the perception, the perceptual presentation or *Vorstellung,* which on being posited becomes the "perceived natural object."

As *Vorstellung* the "perceptual object" is the analogue of the proposition. The perceptual object stands to the perceived natural object as the proposition stands to its corresponding judgment; as the proposition is that which is constituted in judgment and then posited, so the perceptual object is that which is constituted in perception and then posited. We may say accordingly that the perceived natural object reduces to a *Vorstellung.*

This *Vorstellung,* of course, is Husserl's revised version of the traditional "idea." But Husserl, you will recall, modified the traditional view so as to accommodate intentionality with its two performances, constitution and thesis. This entailed the distinction between intending act and intended product, or, which is the same thing, between "idea" as awareness and "idea" as object. The term *"Vorstellung,"* which is usually rendered "presentation" in English but which is also the German word for the traditional "idea," does not clearly connote this distinction; rather it tends to obscure it. To fix the distinction terminologically, Husserl introduces from the Greek the word-pair "noema" (plural: "noemata") and "noesis" (plural: "noeses"). Noema, replacing *Vorstellung,* is the intentionally constituted product or "sense" of an act, its "intentional object." Noesis is the intending, the "intentional act" itself. Noeses are "immanent" in the stream of consciousness; noemata are "transcendent" of the stream. Together they make up the two grand dimensions of consciousness. Henceforth the central theme of Transcendental Phenomenology is that of noesis and noema and their intentional correlation. Thus instead of saying that the perceived natural object reduces to a *Vorstellung,* we shall say that it reduces to a noema.

At this point the analogy between judgment and perception becomes strained. Noemata no longer stand to perceived natural objects as propositions to judgments. Noemata, unlike propositions, are not observable from the natural standpoint; they cannot be perceived. Neither can they be grasped by natural reflection or introspection. Both these operations are carried on in the natural attitude. Because they are not *observable* from the natural standpoint, noemata can only be *thought* in the natural attitude as hypothetical analogues of propositions. But now—so we are assured—these same "theoretical" entities become, by the reduction, "pretheoretical" objects of intuition, immediate data of "transcendental reflection." This means that the reduction is a twofold accomplishment; 1) it reduces perceived objects to unperceivable noemata, and 2) it transforms reflection, increasing its purview by a vast domain of objects, noemata, of which reflection in its natural capacity is utterly oblivious. On both these counts the analogy between perception and judgment, noema and proposition, breaks down. Judgment and proposition are both accessible to natural reflection, and the transition from one to the other entails no transposition of standpoints.

Accordingly, let us abandon this analogy as a key to understanding the reduction, and turn instead to an example in which the reduction is actually carried out. Husserl gives such an example in paragraphs 88 and 89 of the *Ideas.*

Let us assume, he there suggests, that we are in a garden looking at a blossoming apple tree. "In the natural standpoint the apple tree is for us an existing thing in the transcendent reality of space, and the perception . . . is a psychical state be-

longing to us as real people." Now in this kind of situation it
may happen that the perception is a "mere hallucination," that
the perceived apple tree before us does not really exist. In this
event, the "real relation, which was previously meant *(gemeint)*
as really obtaining, is now disturbed. The perception alone remains; there is nothing *real* out there to which it relates" (p. 259).

"Let us now pass over to the phenomenological standpoint. . . .
Together with the whole physical and psychical world the real
obtaining of the real relation between perception and perceived
is suspended; and yet a relation between perception and perceived is obviously left over, a relation which comes to essential
givenness . . . as it fits into the transcendental stream of consciousness [*Erlebnisstrom**]." This latter relation is the intentional relation, now completely divested of any "reality" or "existence," and now seen in its "purity" to obtain whether the perception be genuine or hallucinatory or illusory or deceptive in
any other way. For it is now "evident" that all these modes of
awareness, "in the role they play in the natural standpoint, suc-
cumb to the phenomenological suspension"; their differences fall
away as unessential in the face of the reduction; i.e., they are all
of the same kind: constituting modes of awareness. Hence for
"perception," as for hallucination, there is "no question whether
anything corresponds to it in 'the' reality. This posited (*thetische*)
reality is judgmentally (*urteilsmässig*) simply not there for us.
And yet everything remains, so to speak, as of old. Even the
transcendentally reduced perceptual experience (*Wahrnehmung-
serlebnis*) is the perception of 'this blossoming apple tree, in this
garden, etc.' . . . The tree has suffered not the slightest alteration
in any of its components, qualities, characters . . ." (pp. 259-
260).

In the reduced perception the tree is thus retained intact, but
only as "the perceived as such," as "noema." As such it remains

---

*Erfahrung is "experience"; *Erlebnis* is the "subjective act of experienc-
ing," an occurrence in the stream of consciousness.

in every detail identically the same. In its "existence," however, it is completely other. "The *tree plain and simple,* the thing in nature, is utterly different from the *perceived tree as such,* which as perceptual sense belongs to the perception, and that inseparably. The tree plain and simple can burn away, be resolved into its chemical elements, and so forth. But the sense—the sense of *this* perception, something that necessarily belongs to its essence—cannot burn away; it has no chemical elements, no forces, no real properties"; it is a mere "intentional object" or noema (pp. 260-261).

The difficulty is with the two objects, the two trees, the natural or real tree and the "intentional" tree, the one an object of perception, the other an object of transcendental reflection. In a way the two objects are not two but one. For they are identical in every given detail. And yet, in their "existence" they are as different as can be. The one is out there, capable of bearing fruit, of being cut down and burned, and so on. The other lacks completely these "real," but insensible, properties or potencies; it can do nothing, and can be nothing other than what it is, namely, an intentionally constituted noema or "sense" internal to the perceiving consciousness.

Manifestly the reduction here involves something more than mere existence. For although we may not have altered a single given sensible quality, we have obviously removed all its insensible properties, the inherent powers or dispositions which make up its "essence" as a tree. Suspending existence would thus seem to entail suspending essence as well. Conversely, positing existence would seem to entail positing essence. Even from the transcendental standpoint this is difficult. For it would imply that thesis is not the simple positing of existence, but the constituting of a real essence and infusing it somehow into an already constituted noema, a process which Husserl does not even contemplate.

The nature of such a process we can only conjecture. Noemata are sensible, whereas essences are not. The tree as noema is constituted out of given sensations—"hyletic data," Husserl calls them. The essence of the tree, assuming it to be constituted, must be constituted out of materials insensible in character. We know not what these materials are or how they give rise to essences. Nor do we know how essences are lodged inside noemata and the whole posited as existing out there. All we know is that some such process must take place, if Husserl's theory of reduction is correct; i.e., if noemata are by thesis to become natural objects.

What we learn from the example of the tree is that the positing and suspending of existence is also the positing and suspending of essence; also, that the tree and its noema, the unreduced and the reduced tree, are "identical" in only a very superficial—literally superficial—sense, like the identity of an object with its reflected image, or of a person with his photograph. Of reflection in its two capacities, natural and transcendental, the example of the tree adds nothing to our understanding. Instead, it has added to our perplexity as we contemplate the duality of objects and capacities which result from the reduction—all, of course, considered from the natural standpoint.

I repeat now a former question. Is there actually such a thing as transcendental reflection with noemata as its actual objects? I can discover no such thing, although I once thought I could. But if I can no longer discover it, I can still think it as a consequence flowing from the theory of sensation and ideas and the companion doctrines of constitution and thesis. On this highly theoretical basis alone can I make intelligible Husserl's notion of noemata as objects of a special kind of intuition.

This is to say that the reduction is a theory, an intricate argument, not a piece of phenomenological analysis. It is also to say that the reduction is wholly judgmental, not perceptual or experiential. To assume as Husserl does that perception and experience are "thetic," is to draw once again a false analogy between intellect and sense, like the previous analogy which held that the perceptual synthesis in experience is productive or constitutive like the intellectual synthesis in judgment. The two analogies go closely together and both rest solidly on the theory of sensation and ideas.

Such then is the argument from thesis, or reduction,* the first part of the special argument by which Husserl attempts to show that the outer objects of experience must be internal to consciousness. As an argument, of course, it is fallacious if only because it assumes from the outset what it would prove. Let us now turn to the second part of the special argument which is set forth in the succeeding chapter of the *Ideas*.

B. THE ARGUMENT FROM GIVENNESS

The argument from givenness is quite independent of the argument from thesis and makes no use of the reduction. Beginning once again with what is "given us in the natural attitude (*uns in der natürlichen Einstellung gegeben*)" (p. 112)—the *Lebenswelt* as he later calls it—Husserl seizes on a second insight which, like the first insight, is supplied by this attitude

---

*There are, as every student of the *Ideas* is aware, not one but several "reductions." The fourth chapter of the second section is entitled "The Phenomenological Reductions." Just how many there are is hard to say; but this is of no importance to us here. Important for us is this alone, that the reduction which we have just examined is "fundamental" (*grundlegend*) and prior to all the rest. "The remaining reductions, as presupposing the first, are thus secondary" (p. 179). As presupposing this first reduction the others presuppose a suspending of the general thesis. But beyond this it is not clear how they are properly reductions at all, there being no further theses to suspend. Essences, even "transcendent essences," i.e., essences of transcendent things, are not posited, at least if we mean by positing the conferring of existence, or the "sense" of existing. And if essences are constituted I know of no account thereof, a notable omission in a general theory of constitution. In my opinion, therefore, there is properly but one reduction, the reduction here expounded, and it is to this alone that I refer whenever I use the word "reduction."

yet impels beyond it. This second insight emerges from the following reflections.

Outer objects according to the natural attitude are "real," "existent," "independent." Each of these transcendent objects possesses a "being in itself"; whereas an immanent object (an act or sensation) possesses only a "being in consciousness." But for all this "being in itself" a transcendent object *"is never such as to be out of relation to consciousness and its Ego"* (p. 148); more specifically, it "must needs be experienceable, and not merely by an Ego conjured into being as an empty logical possibility, but by an actual Ego" (p. 150); for *"experienceability, never betokens an empty logical possibility,* but one that has its *motive* in the system of experience" (p. 148).

Husserl begins here by invoking the general argument: transcendent objects must be "related to consciousness." But he proceeds at once to specify: to be related to consciousness is to be "experienceable"; and to be experienceable is to be such as to be "givable" (p. 149). Givenness thus pertains "essentially" to the very being of a transcendent object as experienceable.

Now the mode of givenness characteristic of all sense perception is by way of "perspectives," "adumbrations," or sensuous "appearances," from "points of view," angles of vision, at this or that distance, etc., each *actual* standpoint together with its actual perspectives being, as it were, the momentary focal point of actuality in a limitless "horizon" of *possible* standpoints, each with its own possible perspectives. Each of these possible standpoints—they are manifestly infinite in number—may in turn be actualized, but only one at a time and each time as a fresh center of actuality within this "shifting but everpresent horizon" (p. 149) or "field of perception" (p. 101).

Perceivability or experienceability thus involves 1) givenness in the manner of endlessly varying perspectives of a thing as its appearances, and 2) the perceptual field as the one limitless horizon in which alone all appearances, possible as well as actual, occur—remembering that it is only *actual* perspectives which are *actually* given at any one time. In short, to be transcendent means to be perspectively given (or "givable") within the one field of perception or experience.

This is clear enough. But the picture changes abruptly. The transcendent object with its manifold of actual and possible perspectives or appearances, all occurring in the one field of experience, turns out to be not an objective, but a subjective state of affairs. Actually the change is not abrupt at all; it only seemed abrupt to us. For whereas we had naively taken appearances and perspectives to be *relative* in an empirically real situation, we suddenly realize that Husserl has been taking them all along to be *subjective* sensations internal to consciousness. We learn this on being told that the activity of perceiving a transcendent object is a process of "synthesizing" appearance-manifolds into the unity of a single apprehension, into the one awareness of an identical thing appearing in manifold ways. This "synthesis," obviously subjective, is exercised on a subjective content and issues in a subjective product. Thus, the transcendent object, naively taken to be external to consciousness, must really be internal.

What Husserl has done here is obvious enough by now. He has subjectivized the sense qualities of things, their sensory appearances or perspectives, as the theory of sensation requires. Since these given data are all subjective, the thing thus given must also be subjective, or internal to consciousness. Such, in brief, is the argument from givenness—but only in its opening phase. A second phase follows at once as a kind of corollary.

This corollary has to do with the difference between the outer objects of perception on the one hand and the inner data of introspection—*Erlebnisse* and their immanent contents—on the other hand. This difference is first revealed by the contrast be-

tween their modes of givenness, between a givenness which requires perspectives and a givenness which precludes perspectives. Because inner processes (*Erlebnisse*) cannot appear perspectively, they are by nature "something which *in perception
is given as 'absolute'* " (p. 139). They are "given as 'absolute' "
because they are given not through an endless sequence of
actual and possible perspectives requiring a synthesis which can
never be "complete" (*vollkommen*), but simply, directly, "completely," apodictically. Sense objects, on the other hand, can
only appear through an inexhaustible infinitude of (actual and
possible) perspectives. Patently no outer thing can ever be "completely given"; our perception of it can never be "complete,"
hence the thing can never be given as "absolute."

What Husserl is saying here will boil down eventually to a
pair of statements with which we are already familiar: 1) inner
perception is apodictic whereas outer perception is problematic,
and 2) inner objects are necessary whereas outer objects are
contingent. In the process of arriving at these statements Husserl
leads his reader through a terminological haze where "absolute"
and "complete" double elusively for "necessary" and "apodictic," and where "existence" becomes a function of "givenness."

On penetrating this haze we discern an intelligible, if unacceptable, argument. The argument begins with the assertion of
a "correlation between thing and thing-perception" which is
such that "the sense of thing (*der Sinn von Ding*) gets determined through what is given in thing-perception (and what
else could determine this sense?)" (p. 138). This "correlation"
is intelligible of course only on the assumption of constitution—
an assumption as yet unwarranted, but nonetheless quietly in-
voked. For, manifestly, if the thing is intentionally constituted in
thing-perception, then thing-perception determines the thing or
sense of thing. By virtue of this "correlation," taken now as an
"insight," Husserl infers immediately 1) the necessity of inner

objects from the apodictic quality of inner experience, and 2) the contingency of outer objects from the problematic quality of outer experience.

In a previous chapter I argued that this inferring of existence-quality from experience-quality is simply not valid, that we cannot, for example, infer the necessity of inner existence from the apodictic quality of inner experience. But let us continue with Husserl's argument.

It belongs "to the essence of the thing-world that no perception . . . gives us anything absolute . . . ; and with this hangs essentially together that every . . . experience leaves open the possibility that what is given . . . does *not* exist. It is an essentially valid law that *the existence of a thing is never demanded as necessary by virtue of its givenness,* but in a certain way is always *contingent*" (or "accidental," *zufällig,* p. 144).

To the natural attitude this paragraph is not acceptable. Perception may not "give anything absolute," but this does not "leave open the possibility that what is given [perceived] does not exist." For if only the existent can be perceived (given); then what does not exist cannot be perceived, cannot "really" be given; it can only be a delusion or hallucination. From this it follows analytically that the existence of a perceived thing is always "demanded" as "necessary to its givenness in experience," though not as "necessary in itself," for in itself the perceived is only contingent, exists only contingently.

What Husserl has done here, as I remarked shortly before, is to derive the doctrine of contingent and necessary existence from the doctrine of apodictic and assertoric perception. This is possible only on the assumption of constitution and the "correlation" between thing and thing-perception which it entails. Granted this assumption, then the nature of thing-existence is indeed determined by the nature of thing-perception—at least in the case of outer things. But lacking this assumption, as it was lacking with Descartes, there is no such "correlation" and no possibility of deriving existence from awareness.

Husserl's argument draws to a surprising climax. "In every way, then, it is clear [sic] that everything which is there in the world of things is on grounds of principle *only a presumptive reality (nur präsumptive Wirklichkeit)*; that *I myself,* on the contrary, for whom it is there . . . I myself or my actual experiencings am *absolute* reality, given through a positing (*Setzung*) that is unconditioned and simply inevitable. *The thesis of my pure Ego and its personal life, which is necessary and plainly indubitable, thus stands opposed to the thesis of the world which is contingent. Every bodily (leibhaftig) given thing can also not be; no bodily given experiencing (Erlebnis) can also not be:* that is the essential law which defines this necessity and that contingency" (p. 145).

If positing is imputing existence to something constituted, I do not see how I could posit myself and my actual experiencings, since these include my constitutings and positings of external things. "The thesis of my pure Ego and its personal life" thus sounds very much like a thesis of the general thesis, a positing of positing. Nor do I understand how an "absolute reality" can be "given through a positing that is unconditioned and simply inevitable." A reality or existence that is posited would seem for that very reason to be "presumptive," contingent. And a positing that is in itself unconditioned and inevitable is something quite new and baffling. These obscurities arise in the main from the melange of "absolute," "necessary," "apodictic," "contingent," etc., in which Husserl, unlike Descartes, has confused two very distinct and relatively independent doctrines, the one about existence, the other about evidence—a confusion resulting from Husserl's alleged "correlation" between thing and thing-perception with its tacit assumption of constitution and thesis.

Summarizing: since outer things can be given only perspectively, they cannot be given "adequately" as "absolute" or "necessary," but only as "contingent," i.e., contingent on consciousness, on its operations of constitution and thesis. On the other hand, since inner acts of consciousness cannot be given perspectively, they can be given "adequately" as "absolute" or "necessary." The former is but a corollary to the unstated premise that since the perspectives, through which outer things are given, must be subjective (because relative), the things themselves thus given must also be subjective, or internal to consciousness. The latter follows from the erroneous correlation of existence with evidence.

In reflecting on this argument it is well to remember that we are supposedly "meditating" in the natural attitude on the "motives" that impel beyond it, on the pretheoretical "insights" which lead to the transcendental transposition. Since these motives and insights are supplied by the natural standpoint, we are still on this side of the transposition, this side of the reduction, still working our way toward the new point of view. If we find the going exceedingly rough, it is not only because of the difficulties already encountered. It is also because of further difficulties which arise in the following chapter. The argument from givenness, as I have just sketched it, is but the basis of a more elaborate discussion in which Husserl attempts to consolidate his idealistic position that consciousness is a realm of absolute, necessary being, and, by contrast, natural reality is a realm of contingent, relative being derived from consciousness and internal to it.* This is plainly a discussion of the highest importance for transcendental phenomenology. It harbors further difficulties, of which I shall mention four.

The first of these difficulties is that Husserl seems to hold

*The title of the chapter is "Consciousness and Natural Reality."

that there are primary as well as secondary sensations. Now secondary sensations I find difficult enough to imagine; but I cannot say that they are strictly unintelligible. Impressions of color, sound, smoothness I can envisage with Descartes and the tradition. But impressions—primary impressions—of shape, position, motion, number, and the like I simply cannot envisage. I find them quite unintelligible. With Descartes primary qualities were objective; only secondary qualities were subjective, hence reducible to sensations. Initially there was no thought of primary sensations; sensations, it went without saying, were all secondary. No one, I believe, ever maintained *overtly* that there are primary as well as secondary sensations. This was done only *covertly,* as I remarked in Chapter IV. Husserl never speaks of sensations as primary or secondary, although he frequently speaks of primary and secondary qualities. It is only covertly that he holds to primary as well as secondary sensations. This he does in his emphatic insistence that perceived sense qualities are in every instance to be distinguished sharply from their corresponding unperceived sensations or appearances.

"Like the perceived thing generally, so all its parts, sides, and components, be they primary or secondary qualities, are also necessarily transcendent of the perception, and on the same grounds everywhere. The color of the thing seen is in principle not a real [*reel*] component of the consciousness of color: it [the color] appears, but while appearing the appearance can and *must* be continually changing, as experience shows. The *same* color appears 'in' continuous manifolds of *color-perspectives*. Similarly for every other sense quality and likewise for every spatial shape! One and the same shape . . . appears continuously ever again 'in another way,' in ever differing shape-perspectives" (pp. 130-131).

Notice that Husserl, like Berkeley, finds primary and secondary qualities occurring inseparably together and enjoying the same status. Unlike Berkeley, however, he distinguishes sharply between perceived sense quality and unperceived sensation, or quality-perspective. This distinction looks very much like the distinction between transcendent thing and its noema. But Husserl does not speak here of reducing transcendent qualities to immanent sensations as their noemata. Reduction to noemata was the theme of the previous chapter. The theme of the present chapter is givenness, which he is attempting to treat quite independently of the former. He finds that he does not have to invoke the reduction and so refrains from all mention of noemata. Accordingly, instead of object and noema, he speaks of "quality" and its "perspectives." *"The perspective [Abschattung] though called by the same name is in principle not of the same genus as what is perspected [Abgeschattetes].* A perspective is a subjective occurrence (*Erlebnis*). But *Erlebnis* is possible only as *Erlebnis,* not as something spatial. What is perspected, however, is in principle possible only as something spatial (it is indeed in essence spatial) but not possible as *Erlebnis*. In particular it is also nonsense to take the shape-perspective (e.g., that of a triangle) for something spatial and capable of being in space, and whoever does this is confusing it with the perspected, i.e., appearing shape" (p. 132).

The last remark that a shape-perspective is not itself something spatial is surprising. If the perspective of a triangle, for instance, is not another triangle or a straight line, i.e., something manifestly spatial, then I do not know what it could be— save possibly a primary sensation or impression! Husserl seems to have been carried away at this point by the force of his contention that we must distinguish "in principle" between the transcendent color, say, and the immanent color-perspective (the sensation) and in exactly the same way between a transcendent shape and the immanent shape-perspective. Now if the color-perspective is a subjective sensation, is not also the shape-perspective a subjective sensation? Are there not, in other words, primary sensations or impressions just as there are secondary sensations or impressions?

The implication is unmistakable. To every perceived quality of an object, both primary and secondary, there correspond in the perceiving subject immanent sensory contents which are "the perspectives of color, shape, and so forth. They are counted among the *'sensory data' [Empfindungsdaten]*, data . . . which combine into concrete unities of experience; which, further . . . within the concrete unity of perception are animated [*beseelt*] through *'apprehensions' [Auffassungen]* and in this animation [*Beseelung*] exercise the *'presenting [darstellende] function'* or in unison with it make up what we call the 'appearing of' color, shape, and so forth" (pp. 131-132).

Notice the repeated pairing here of color and shape, the one a secondary, the other a primary quality, with the plain implication that there are corresponding secondary *and* primary sensations—which, indeed, is quite necessary if *all* perceived qualities are to have their immanent perspectives or appearances in the perceiving act.

Notice, too, that the immanent sensuous appearances of the transcendent qualities are not themselves sensations, but "contain" sensations. For sensations *"in themselves contain nothing of intentionality,"* (p. 247) and hence cannot serve as perspectives or appearances of anything; they are but raw nonintentional materials, "hyletic data." As such, however, they can "enter into intentional functions"; they can be "animated through apprehension [*Auffassung*]," and in this sense intentionalized. Only when thus "animated" or intentionalized do they become appearances of color, shape, smoothness, etc., i.e., perspectives in the proper sense. A manifold of these immanent (sensuous) perspectives is then synthesized in a single "unity of apprehension," and we perceive a transcendent color or shape or smoothness. Finally, by a further synthesis we combine transcendent color, shape, and smoothness into the unity of a perceived transcendent object.

It is interesting to note here how casually Husserl treats of the initial processing of sensations. In Chapter V, I argued that this initial processing entails transformation and projection through which the raw sensations acquire, among other things, "extensity"—a splendid euphemism for "rendering spatial what must be in principle nonspatial"! To all of this Husserl pays only the slightest heed, as though it did not need, or merit, investigation. He simply condenses it into the curious metaphor of "animation"; raw nonintentional sensations are "animated through apprehension" and are thus made to "enter into intentional functions." I find this quite incomprehensible; although I must confess that I find it no more mystifying than transformation and projection—and extensity! So much, then, for the first difficulty.

The second difficulty has to do with Husserl's notion of "thing" (*Ding*). He uses this term throughout the present chapter in a way that is quite baffling to the reader. Initially *Ding* plainly signifies "object" as distinct from its "qualities," primary and secondary, as in the passages just quoted. But as the chapter progresses *Ding* comes gradually to signify both "object and quality"—or perhaps "object-with-its-qualities"—in a manner which completely glosses over the important distinction between object and quality and the relation between them. With the disappearance of this distinction confusion ensues.

Taking as basic the distinction between object and quality, the order of constitution, as we just noted, would be distinctly threefold: 1) hyletic data, primary and secondary sensations, are converted by "animation" into immanent perspectives; 2) a manifold of immanent perspectives, potentially infinite in number, is perceived by synthesis as a single transcendent quality (a color or shape); and 3) a manifold of transcendent qualities presumably finite in number, is perceived by a further synthesis as a transcendent object (the colored and shaped thing). This threefold schema would appear to be clear enough. But it is not. It harbors a number of equivocations.

Notice first the two senses of "transcendence," the one referring to the transcendence of the object, and the other to the transcendence of its qualities, these being presumably two distinct orders of transcendence. Corresponding to these two senses and orders of transcendence we should naturally expect two equally distinct orders of synthesis, the one giving us qualities and the other the (qualified) object. Manifestly these two senses of "synthesis" and "transcendence" must be clearly distinguished if ambiguity is to be avoided. Similarly with "appearance" and "appearance manifold"; they too are equivocal. In one of its senses "appearance" refers to immanent perspective as appearance of a transcendent quality; in another it refers to a transcendent quality as appearance of a transcendent object. Since "appearance" and "appearance manifold" refer on the one hand to something *immanent* and on the other to something *transcendent,* their equivocation calls for extra caution. And the more so when we reflect that whereas an appearance manifold of immanent perspectives is potentially infinite, an appearance manifold of transcendent qualities would seem to be strictly finite.

Although the schema of constitution rests on the distinction between object and quality, the schema tends to fade away as this distinction vanishes in the notion of *Ding.* Under the darkening aegis of *Ding* the two orders of transcendence and synthesis merge indistinguishably into one. The important relation between object and quality is lost to view. We cannot tell whether or not qualities are appearances of objects, indices perhaps of their essences, as I suggested in the instance of the apple tree. Nor can we tell whether or not the qualities of things are finite in number.

We do know that the immanent appearance manifolds of given qualities are potentially infinite. But beyond this we are quite uncertain; the above equivocations have become ambiguities.

Most striking of all, perhaps, is the circumstance that although Husserl distinguishes repeatedly the transcendent object from its transcendent qualities,* yet he never once, to my knowledge, characterizes the object or its constitution in terms of its qualities or of its relations to its qualities. The only terms he uses are those of "appearance," "perspective," "adumbration," terms which apply directly only to qualities. I repeat: it is only qualities that can literally appear. Immanent appearance manifolds, consisting of animated hyletic data, are perspectives of qualities, not of objects. Now it may well be argued that since qualities are qualities of objects, perspectives of qualities must also be perspectives of objects. But argument here is out of place, phenomenological analysis and clarification are called for. All Husserl has shown is that qualities, not objects, appear in immanent perspectives. How objects also appear we are not told; although it would seem to be through their sensible qualities. But this is no longer a question for Husserl. Object and quality have been swallowed up in the notion of *Ding*. Thus he simply assures us that the transcendent *Ding*—object or quality or both?—is nothing but an "identity of appearance-modes through adumbration [*Identisches von Erscheinungsweisen durch Abschattung*]" (p. 139), hence that the being of the transcendent *Ding* is, "according to its sense [*Sinn*], a mere intentional being," a being "which consciousness in its experiencings posits [*setzt*], which in principle is intuitable and determinable as an identity of . . . appearance manifolds—but *over and above this* nothing at all" (p. 153).

The denouement of this doctrine of *Ding* as an "identity of

*In addition to the passages already quoted see p. 161, where Husserl speaks of "the thing that appears to sense, which has the sensory properties of shape, color, smell and taste. . . ." This is all repeated at length in pp. 364 through 366.

appearance manifolds" occurs in Husserl's contention that the transcendent thing must be an "Idea,"—not an "idea" in the traditional sense, but an "Idea" (with a capital "I") in the sense of Kant's Transcendental Dialectic. Whether an "appearance manifold" be a manifold of immanent perspectives or of transcendent qualities, it includes in every instance more than any actually given set of appearances here and now. It comprehends not only present but also past and future appearances, not only actual but also possible appearances, infinitely numerous in the case of immanent perspectives, finitely numerous (presumably) in the case of transcendent qualities. In both cases—although perhaps only or chiefly in the first—the manifold cannot "in principle" ever be completely or "adequately" given. With respect to its givenness it must always remain incomplete, "inadequate." Consequently, the "identity" of that which is thus given —the thing as identity of appearance manifolds—must be only an ideal limit which, in the order of givenness, experience can approach but never attain. It must be, in a word, a Kantian "Idea" (p. 240) which it would be absurd to take as "real."*

My third difficulty is that this notion of *Ding* as Idea appears to be sharply at odds with the doctrine of the reduction. Remember, this notion together with all that leads up to it is available to the natural standpoint, pretheoretically evident to natural reflection. Prior to the reduction we can discover that what we unreflectively take to be "real" is actually "ideal." There was no hint of this when we considered the blossoming apple tree standing before us in the fullness of its perceptual presence, no intimation that over and beyond its perceptual presence the tree was in fact an ideal identity of appearance manifolds. Taking the tree simply as it presented itself, just as it was actually given,

*Notice that "like the thing [*Ding*] every quality . . . is an Idea" (pp. 414-415). Does this suggest that the qualities are *not* potentially infinite in number?

we suspended its existence and reduced it to a "perceived as such," to a noema, identical in every given detail with the tree as natural object. Now, however, we learn that the tree was not the "reality" we took it to be, but an "ideality" of which we were quite unaware. All this, mind you, in the natural attitude!

Manifestly there is something wrong. If the tree is an Idea, and known to be such, then it cannot possibly be posited as real, existing, natural; for these are precisely the predicates which à Kantian Idea precludes in principle. Even assuming it to have been posited—*per impossibile*—it cannot possibly be reduced to a "perceived as such" identical in every given detail with the unreduced original. For the unreduced original, the Idea, not only exceeds the momentarily given details, it also differs from these latter in kind: it is intelligible and abiding whereas the given details are sensuous and fleeting. Moreover, as Idea it would seem to be in its unreduced form already a kind of noema or *Vorstellung,* thus rendering the reduction superfluous as well as impossible.

On the other hand, if we take the tree as real, unmindful of its ideality, then its reduction is at least conceivable, also its previous positing, as we saw in the section on the reduction. But then we are faced with the question of the relation between the tree as intelligible Idea and as sensible reality, since it seems to be both for Husserl. This relation, as I make it out, would appear to be that of container to contained: the intelligible Idea somehow contains the real as a shifting sensuous "core" of actuality, a manifold momentarily given, the tree just as it is perceived here and now. This would make the Idea a limit which experience can only approximate; but it would also make it an ideal totality which somehow contains its successive "cores" as integral parts of itself. This is exceedingly difficult to grasp. For it is not at all clear how an Idea, any more than a class, can thus literally contain its members. One class can literally contain another, at least in the fashion of class-inclusion. But a class cannot in the same sense contain its members; the class-inclusion relation is simply different in kind from the class-membership relation. We can only conclude that the relation between the tree as Idea and as real cannot be that of container to contained. What else it might be Husserl does not even intimate.

Thus if the tree is real—hence reducible—it is hard to see how it can also be an Idea. If it be an Idea, it is hard to see how it can be reduced—or posited. In either event, Husserl's doctrine of *Ding* as Idea, as ideal identity of appearance manifolds, is unclear both in itself and in its relation to the reduction.

Also difficult to square with the reduction is Husserl's notion of the "field" or "horizon" of perception. In the natural attitude this field or horizon is the space of the world. As empirical it presumably exists in some sense and hence can be reduced—to a noema? If to a noema, is this noema intentionally constituted in a corresponding noesis? And if constituted, out of what is it wrought? If it does not reduce to a noema, then what precisely is it, and what is its relation to intentional consciousness with its noesis-noema complex?

Husserl does not raise or answer these questions. He seems to have concealed them from himself by an artful choice of terms. Rarely, if ever, does he speak of the "empirical space of the world"; he speaks rather of the "field" or "horizon of perception," thereby insinuating that this field or horizon is as subjective as perception itself. Thus he simply adduces the field as self-evident, which it is, and as self-evidently subjective, which it is not. It is subjective for Husserl solely because its inhabitants, the sensible qualities of things, have been declared subjective by the theory of sensation. This is my fourth and final difficulty.

If I have been tediously long in stating these difficulties, it is chiefly because I have found it exceedingly hard to disentangle the profusion and confusion of themes and arguments which make up this involved chapter on givenness. The upshot of these difficulties is, of course, that the arguments of this chapter are untenable. Granting that external objects can be given only perspectively, it does not follow that these perspectives are subjective and hence that outer objects must be subjectively constituted as identities of appearance manifolds. Granting, too, that inner acts preclude spatial perspectives and can be given apodictically, whereas outer objects requiring perspectives cannot be given apodictically, it does not follow that acts are given as "necessary" and consciousness as "absolute reality," whereas objects are given as "contingent" on a positing by consciousness. I cannot grant that there are primary as well as secondary sensations, or that "animation" is anything more than a dubious metaphor. Nor can I grant that object and quality are to be merged indistinguishably in *Ding,* or that *Ding* must be somehow both intelligible Idea and sensible reality, both irreducible and reducible. Finally, I cannot grant that the empirical space of the world is but a subjective "horizon" of perception.

It is time now to review the special argument as a whole and the "insights" which supply its premises. The special argument, you will recall, is special in that it treats of a specific mode of intentional consciousness, namely, outer or sense perception; whereas the general argument treats only of intentional consciousness in general. The aim of the special argument, like that of the general, is to show that external objects must be internal to consciousness, hence must be subjectively constituted and posited. The "insights" that lead to this conclusion are principally these. One, the "essence" of the natural standpoint is a "general thesis" whereby external things are said to exist. Two, external things must be given perspectively, whence they must be constituted as identities of appearance manifolds. The first insight I denied outright; the second I granted but denied the conclusion. A third insight, a kind of corollary of number two, is that inner acts can be given apodictically, hence consciousness exists necessarily. This "insight," too, I granted but denied the conclusion. Finally there is the "insight" of the general argument, that the world on becoming "related" to consciousness becomes thereby internal to consciousness—because the intentional relation is internal to its object. This insight I denied altogether. The upshot of all this is that the natural standpoint supplies no insights or motives which impel beyond it; the transcendental standpoint is a theoretical fiction.

As we survey these arguments it becomes increasingly evident that Husserl's "insights" have all been refracted through one primordial "insight," the theory of sensation. Husserl never speaks of the theory of sensation as such and never recognizes it even obliquely as the primary source of the whole transcendental outlook. It is for him not a theory. Sensations, sense impressions, sense data, are for him not theoretical assumptions, but pretheoretical certainties which it never occurs to him to question. Since he does not question them, he offers no phenomenological exposition which would clarify, let alone justify, their assumption. Although he mentions them frequently from the third of the *Logical Investigations* on, it is in a single paragraph of the *Ideas,* paragraph 85, that he treats of them explicitly. Let us close this section on Husserl with a brief look at this paragraph on "hyletic data."

C. HYLETIC DATA

In the general domain of intentional consciousness there is a radical distinction to be drawn between two kinds of experiencings (*Erlebnisse*): 1) those that are *"sensual which in themselves contain nothing of intentionality,"* and 2) those "that bear the specific quality of intentionality" (p. 247). The first stands to the second as "matter" or "stuff" to "form," as "sensual ὕλη" to "intentional μορφή." Husserl does not here decide whether or not sensual contents are invariably subject to "animating apprehensions" [*beseelende Auffassungen*], and thus invariably enter into "intentional functions," nor whether or not intentionality requires in every instance a sensory foundation. He simply remarks that the whole domain of intentional consciousness is dominated by this "remarkable duality and unity of *sensual ὕλη* and *intentional μορφή*" (ibid.).

This duality and unity is especially conspicuous in the region of sense perception or external experience. Here the terms "sensory" or "sensuous" are used in a narrower and proper sense to "signify the phenomenological residuum of what in normal outer perception is mediated through the 'senses'" (p. 248), namely such "'sensory contents' as color-data, touch-data, sound-data, and the like,* which we shall no longer confuse with the appearing phases of things, their color-quality, roughness, etc.," qualities which "by means of these data 'present' themselves in our experiencings" (p. 246). We as phenomenologists are spared this "confusion" of sense data with sense qualities by our recognition of intentionality. We can now see—as our predecessors could not see, for lack of intentionality—that the nonintentional sense data, sensations, impressions must first be intentionalized, i.e., "animated through apprehensions," before they can become intentional appearances or perspectives *of* things (more precisely, *of* the transcendent sense qualities of things). Thus it is clear to us how these raw, nonintentional sense data "offer themselves as the materials [*Stoffe*] for intentional formations or sense-bestowings of different levels" and how they are "to be found as components in more compre-

---

*Notice that this list contains only secondary "data" or impressions, no primary data or impressions.

hensive concrete experiencings [*Erlebnisse*] which as wholes are intentional, and indeed so that over these sensory components lies, as it were, an 'animating,' *sense-bestowing* stratum . . . , a stratum through which, out of the sensory that in itself contains nothing of intentionality, the concrete intentional experience |*Erlebnis*| comes to pass" (p. 247; cf. also pp. 283f.).

In introducing the term "hyletic data" Husserl makes it clear that this term is of wider extension than the term "sense data." "Hyletic data" embraces the sensory in general, including besides the traditional sensations such sensory impressions as those of pleasure, pain, tickling, kinesthetic sensations, and the like, also such sensory occurrences as impulses, feelings, and emotions in the sphere of will. Sense data (sensations) are thus a sub-genus of hyletic data, that sub-genus which refers only to the "phenomenological residuum of that which is mediated through the 'senses' in normal outer perception. Subsequent to the reduction an essential affinity between the relevant 'sensory' data of the external intuitions reveals itself, and there corresponds to it a unique generic essence, a fundamental concept of phenomenology" (p. 248). Obviously, this "unique genus" embraces only what have here been called from the outset "sensations," the sensations proper to the theory of sensation. It does not refer in any way to other genera of sensory data such as those that occur in feeling and will. We must remember therefore that although all sense data are hyletic data, not all hyletic data are sense data.

In correlating sensory ὕλη and intentional μορφή Husserl is in effect making the hyletic a counterpart of the intentional, the two being the primary components of consciousness as *Erlebnis*. It would seem inevitable, therefore, that a science of hyletics should accompany and complement the science of intentionality. "Naturally *pure hyletics* falls under the phenomenology of transcendental consciousness. It has, moreover, the character of a self-contained discipline, and has as such its own value; however, from the functional standpoint it derives its significance from the fact that it offers possible interweavings [*Einschläge*] with the intentional fabric, possible materials [*Stoffe*] for intentional formations. Not only as regards difficulty, but also as regards the relative rank of the problems from the standpoint of the idea of absolute knowledge, it stands clearly below noetic and functional phenomenology" (pp. 253-254). Important though it may be, "pure hyletics" is yet only secondary to the main theme of transcendental phenomenology. Only to the extent that hyletic data are involved in the noesis-noema complex is their mention unavoidable. In the writings of Husserl there is no further development of a science or discipline of "hyletics."

Such a science of "hyletics" would undertake, among other things, a comprehensive inventory of sense data and thus come to grips with the problem of primary and secondary sensations. As it is, we have no such inventory and no dealing with the problem. We have only clues. In this section, where something more might well be expected, we have but two listings, both typically brief. In the first, as quoted above, Husserl mentions only three—color data, touch data, and sound data—all of them secondary sensations. A few paragraphs later he charges Brentano with failing to distinguish, in his notion of "physical phenomena," between "sense data" and that which "appears" in these data, "the color of a thing, the shape of a thing, and the like" (p. 250). The context clearly suggests that corresponding to shape there is a shape-sensation, as to color a color-sensation, which on being animated becomes an immanent shape-perspective, as the color-sensation becomes an immanent color-perspective. This is as far as the evidence goes; but here as elsewhere it points unfailingly to an unexpressed belief in primary as well as secondary sensations.

Another problem for a science of "hyletics" would be the cause or source of sensations. Are they but brute facts of inexplicable origin, irrational surds in an otherwise rational system of intentionality? Or are they, too, in the last analysis, intentional products? Also, what actually takes place when sensations are "animated" by intentionality? Will we find, behind this metaphor of "animation," the remarkable processes of transformation and projection which I discussed in Chapter V? Still another problem would be that of the relation between sensations and the other genera of hyletic data. Are these other genera also animated? If so, how? If not, why not? And so on.

If Husserl was aware of these difficulties, it was only in passing. He was content to mention the mere possibility of a science of hyletics. He was content with this because the issues of this science are trivial in comparison with those of "intentional phenomenology." He was content for another and more compelling reason: hyletics would deal with a matter which has long been settled and established by the traditional theory of sensation.

This is all that we are told about sense data. In substance it is but a repetition of what Husserl has been saying ever since the third of the *Logical Investigations,* if not before. Without doubt or question he simply assumes sensations and, with them, also constitution, thesis, synthesis, and all the other items "sedimented" in this great thought and language complex. In appropriating this traditional complex, to be sure, Husserl made one great innovation; he intentionalized consciousness. With this he wrought a vast change in the complex as a whole and introduced a host of refinements in its details, all as a consequence of making intentionality the primary agency of constitution and thesis.

And so, in Husserl's doctrine of "hyletic data" the theory of sensation has found what may be its last refuge. Here, as in other lurking places, it provided the central "insight" from which the others follow in train. Or, if not an insight, then the initial impulse which set in flight a speculative theory, whose soaring trajectory we have been following in this essay. Its principal stages are those of sensations, ideas, constitution, thesis, and monadism—with Husserl, a monadism as absolute as any in the history of thought. One item alone is not at home in this trajectory: intentionality. It was the absence of *intentio,* as much as anything else, which allowed Descartes originally to launch his theory of sensation and ideas. Its later introduction is, historically speaking, an afterthought. In making intentionality the sustaining thrust of the sensation theory Husserl gave to the theory a new impetus. But he gave intentionality a wrenching blow; he capped its open end, clamped it securely between noesis and noema, and made of it at once a prisoner and a prop of monadism.

This is to say that in joining *intentio* to the sensation theory Husserl injured only *intentio*. He has shown us thereby that *intentio* must be liberated from the theory of sensation, that it must be treated in its own right as a genuine "phenomenon," a phenomenon worth "saving." With the insight that the intentional relation is not internal at both ends, but external at the object end, a fresh start can be made toward a phenomenology of perception and experience that shall be truly free of theoretical predilections—free, at least, of the amazing theory of sensation and the monadism which it entails.

VIII
Conclusion: The Purge

Quite apart from its truth or falsity the theory of sensation has played a momentous historic role. With the advent of this theory modern philosophy began, striking out on a strange new path, which in the main it has followed for three centuries. Shortly after its first appearance the sensation theory shed its identity as a theory and assumed the guise of a pretheoretical certainty. In this guise it found obscurity in the murky background of the theory of ideas and of its companion piece, monadism. With ideas and monadism thus in tow the theory of sensation became the sovereign predilection which supplied the framework and ground rules for philosophizing in the modern vein, from Descartes to Husserl, much as revelation supplied the framework and ground rules for philosophizing in the medieval vein. Doubtless the time will come when the historian of philosophy on looking back will find the "modern" prepossession with sensations no less strange than the medieval prepossession with revelation.

In playing this sovereign role the sensation theory committed modern philosophy to a program of speculative theorizing. This speculative program has one central theme: how on the basis of sensations to account for scientific knowledge and how to overcome the monadic dualism which the theory of sensation

154

entails. In placing this theme beyond the reach of inquiry modern philosophy in effect abandoned inquiry and gave itself over to the free construction of hypothetical systems. From the ensuing display of speculative ingenuity arose the many "isms" which make up the distinctive fabric of modern philosophy: idealism, empiricism, parallelism, materialism, pragmatism, phenomenalism, behaviorism, and the like, all of them but variations on the one central theme.

In one respect the most interesting of these variations is that of transcendental phenomenology. For it introduced into the traditional framework an alien element, intentionality, the very absence of which had made possible the inception of the sensation theory. In construing the relation of sensations to outer things as that of inner effects to outer causes, not that of awareness to object, Descartes substituted a causal relation for the intentional relation. This substitution was bound to be threatened when Brentano and Husserl revived intentionality and strove to fit it into the modern framework. But the threat was no less great to intentionality. For the two are so incompatible that one must yield to the other. With Brentano and Husserl intentionality gave way and suffered accordingly. It is now time, I submit, that the sensation theory give way to intentionality.

This is to imply, of course, that the theory of sensation is quite untenable. It is also to suggest that modern philosophy from Descartes to Husserl has been a monumental fallacy. This is a harsh verdict and far too sweeping. No great movement of thought can be thus summarily indicted. Fortunately, modern philosophy had other bases than the sensation theory and other interests than those of epistemology. Obviously the movement as a whole cannot be brought under this indictment, only that segment which derives directly from the theory of sensation. This segment, however, is so central and so large that its removal is bound to entail a vast renovation of the whole edifice.

There are signs that such a renovation is in the making, that speculation is giving way to inquiry. There is a growing suspicion of sense data. "Idea" has fallen into disuse, as though debased by its inherent ambiguity. Even monadism, the most stubbornly ingrained of all, appears on occasion to be relaxing the grim hold which it has taken on the modern mind. Heartening as all this is, it is not enough. Repudiation must be explicit. The whole complex must be disowned and with it the language which it has spawned, the language of sensations, which has become in effect the *lingua franca* of modern philosophy. In this language and its rules of use the sensation theory is so deeply sedimented as to become a vast predilection, a set of fixed habits of expression and thought. Here lies the sinister power of the tradition. Here is where the unwary is most likely to be betrayed and to relapse into the Cartesian malady.

To cure this Cartesian malady, to purge us of the incubus of sensations, would seem to be one of the aims implicit in the turn which contemporary philosophy has taken. Curiously, this turn was foreshadowed by Husserl himself in the great work of his later years, *Die Krisis der Europäischen Wissenschaften.* Here at the close of his career Husserl returned to the *Lebenswelt,* this time however not with the design of neutralizing and reducing it, as in the *Ideas,* so that he might abandon it for the transcendental realm, but with the design of probing its inner depths, its many-layered structures or "sedimentations," so that he might recover the primal insights which gave rise to modern natural science and philosophy. In this penetrating inquiry into the "genesis" of modern thought Husserl led phenomenology away from speculation into the path of investigation.*

---

*It is a pleasure at long last to say something favorable of Husserl. From my negative criticisms one might infer that I owe him nothing. Quite the contrary. My debt to Husserl is immense, as is evident on every page of this essay. If I have felt free to criticize unsparingly his transcendental phenomenology, it is chiefly because the genetic phenomenology of the *Krisis* has showed me another and better way.

Heidegger, if I understand him at all, is relentlessly pursuing this course. He has completely abandoned transcendental phenomenology for genetic phenomenology. But the source which he is seeking lies even deeper than that of modern science and philosophy; it is the primordial insights or revelations that underlie the whole life of man, the life of mind passionately striving, in its encounter with "beings" to detect and express the deeper reverberations of "Being" itself.

From Husserl existentialism, too, has absorbed a profound concern for the *Lebenswelt* and is desperately at pains to lay bare its hidden sense and structure. To this end Sartre retains the reduction and so far reverts to transcendental phenomenology. But his reversion is also an alteration. For what the reduction discloses to Sartre is not a sublime transcendental ego but a terrible freedom of consciousness not only to disengage itself from a world it has constituted but, more imperatively, to recover this engagement, now recognized as an awesome task. In this highly ethical and activist context constitution is but a moment in an agonizing exercise of freedom, an inescapable mandate to transform self and society, even though by the conditions of that effort one is condemned to fail. As existence is prior to essence, so ethics is prior to ontology. And frustration is the crown of authentic existence—or so it would seem.

Merleau-Ponty, too, reverts to the reduction. But what the reduction reveals to him is not a transcendental consciousness, pure or empty; it is rather a consciousness so wedded to the world that it cannot even in idea disengage itself therefrom. The effort to disengage (the reduction) brings to awareness with finality the inextricable involvement of consciousness with the world, an involvement which is one with the existence of consciousness. Thus the reduction reveals the transcendence of the world, rather than that of consciousness. The inalienable presence of the world is manifest in perception, through which we find ourselves in the *Lebenswelt* with its characteristic confusion and profusion, neither wholly senseless nor wholly sensible, rather "ambiguous." To live in this ambiguity, to labor at its unending resolution, is to live in the secular world of history, as perforce we must. Philosophy is but a more acute awareness of this existential involvement.

From quite another side, a side where empirical rather than metaphysical motives tend to prevail, the *Lebenswelt* has moved covertly to the fore. I refer to linguistic analysis, which has found in language the key to philosophic understanding. The great promise of this movement lies in its growing tendency to see in language not only a "game" with its "rules of use," but also and more importantly a luminous access to *rerum natura,* a great refracting medium, so to speak, through which man and nature come philosophically into view, as Plato pointed out long ago. The "language game" would then be seen to be virtually one with the great game of life itself. For language is in sooth the most distinctive creation of the natural attitude and its proper vehicle. Language is the *Lebenswelt* rendered articulate. As such it is a genuine *prius,* a genuine pretheoretical basis for philosophical inquiry. Also, the very use of language would seem to commit us to the "realism" of the *Lebenswelt* with a finality which precludes any "suspension" with its illusory "transposition of standpoints."

Thus, from many sides contemporary philosophy seems to be converging on the *Lebenswelt* as though impelled by a common aim to return to the living center of human existence and value. Here, if anywhere, is the source of that understanding which will permit philosophy once again to enter into the mainstream of our feverish existence and to address itself to "the real business and fortunes of the human race." If the mood of this aim is militantly secular, its secularism is not doctrinaire, not that of a preemptive formula religious or philosophical. Hence it is not inherently opposed to a possible life beyond the grave nor to a possible transcendence with which we must ultimately reckon. It is opposed, however, to allowing our preoccupation with these possibilities to interfere with the pressing business at hand: the "relief of man's estate" through a conquest of nature in which all may share. Life this side of the grave can no longer be deferred.

If this be genuinely the aim which more or less unconsciously is drawing philosophy back to the *Lebenswelt* after three centuries of wandering in the wasteland of sensations, it is none other than the grand motive which originally gave birth to the world we call "modern," the motive of scientific humanism. In contemporary philosophy this motive would seem to be reasserting itself, calling for a return to sober inquiry after the long orgy of speculative theorizing initiated by Descartes. The brew which sustained this orgy was concocted of sensations, ideas, and monadism. If we are to eschew this brew, we must purge its noxious ingredients.

Just such a purge seems to be in the making: not as a project in its own right, but as the concomitant of a new spirit of inquiry impelled by a new sense of urgency. In this ferment we appear to be returning to the wellsprings of western thought. From this fresh stirring of the waters a truly classical revival may emerge—if, indeed, it is not already upon us.

INDEX

acts: and individuality, 58-60; as intending, 96; other than object, 102; "real" and "intentional," 104-106

anticipation: role in time-synthesis, 84

Aquinas, St. Thomas: and *influxus physicus,* 12

Aristotle: and *physis,* 12; categories of accident, 23; primacy of knowledge of things, 103; soul becomes object known, 106

atomism, psychological: in Berkeley, Locke, Hume, 47

awareness: and object, 43; modes of, 49-50; and intentionality, 101-102

Bacon, Francis: on knowledge and power, 20-21

Berkeley, George: primary-secondary qualities, 7, 46-48; on ideas, 36; attacks causal premise, 40; and Husserl, 138-39; mentioned, 9

Brentano, Franz: teacher of Husserl, 97

Burtt, Edwin A.: on primary-secondary qualities, 14-15

Cassirer, Ernst: on primary-secondary qualities, 14-15

certainty: modes of, 55-57

Chardin, Teilhard de: and "noosphere," 92, 107

consciousness: non-monadic character of, 103, 106; as act and object (Husserl), 110-11, 119, 121; world related to (Husserl), 116-17

constitution: and sensation, 94; and theory of sensation, 98, and radical monadism (Husserl), 111; and positing (Husserl), 119; and perception (Husserl), 135

Descartes, René: and theory of sensation, 4, 13, 14, on *res cogitans* and *res extensa,* 8-12; argument on qualities, 34-35; and modes of awareness, 50-58; apodictic evidence, 61; on contingent and necessary, 64-65; on existence and experience, 67-71; intentional relation, 108; and suspension of existence, 125

empiricists, British: formulation of theory of sensation, 35

Erlebnisse (Husserl): given absolutely, 133-34; nonspatial, 139; two kinds of, 148-53

essence: in conceiving things, 63; suspension of (Husserl), 129; notion of (Husserl), 131*n*

evidence: apodictic, assertoric, problematic, 53-57; assertoric and actual existence, 66; apodictic and problematic (Husserl), 134-35

161